ONCE UPON A KITCHEN

101 MAGICAL RECIPES

Get Creative 6
19 West 21st Street, Suite 601
New York, NY 10010

Library of Congress Cataloging-in-Publication Data
Bilderback, Leslie, author.
Once upon a kitchen: 101 magical recipes / Leslie Bilderback.
Description: First edition. | New York : Get Creative 6, 2021. | Includes index.
Identifiers: LCCN 2019058208 | ISBN 9781640210707 (hardcover)
Subjects: LCSH: Cooking--History. | LCGFT: Literary cookbooks.
Classification: LCC TX645 .B55 2021 | DDC 641.509--dc23
LC record available at https://lccn.loc.gov/2019058208
Printed in Singapore.

3 5 7 9 10 8 6 4 2

sixthandspring.com

Photography, Teri Lyn Fisher

Editor, Pamela Wissman

Art Director, Joe Vior

Production, J. Arthur Media

Chief Executive Officer
Caroline Kilmer

President
Art Joinnides

Chairman
Jay Stein

Dedication

Once again, I'm dedicating this book to my family:

To Bill, who exposed me to so much of this source material (mostly, he just watched it,
and I tried to join in, because I thought he was cute, and I wanted him to like me).

To Emma, who, although she shares my DNA, is very much her father's daughter,
and helped me flesh out the Shakespeare, *Star Wars*, and Disney ideas that I struggled with.

To Claire, my eternal cheerleader—I could be writing a book on anything, and she would encourage me.

And finally to Kristi, my mommy, who finally lives close enough
to share in the daily angst of a writer.

ONCE UPON A KITCHEN

101 MAGICAL RECIPES

INSPIRED BY STAR WARS, HARRY POTTER, MERLIN, TOLKIEN, FAIRY TALES, AND MORE

LESLIE BILDERBACK

Get Creative 6

Contents

Cooking is Magic!

...But not in the way many chefs want you to believe. It's not technical or difficult. It doesn't require a cooking degree. I should know. I've been a professional chef for thirty years, and I have that degree. But if there is one thing I have learned in all that time, it's that anyone can cook.

But cooking *is* magic in the way it makes you feel that you've created something special. It's magic in the way it makes your friends and family feel that someone cares enough to make them an amazing meal. It's magic in the way it brings people together over breakfast, at a barbeque, or in line at a food truck. And it's magic in the way it will unite a culture around a traditional bread or a common spice blend or a national holiday.

I was thinking about this culinary magic when I began writing *Once Upon a Kitchen*. I knew there were others like me, with a similar infatuation with the fantastic, the magical, the enchanted. And I thought, "Wouldn't it be great to share a meal with them?" So that's what I did. I imagined dinner parties with like-minded devotees of all my favorite genres—fantasy, literature, history, movies, television, science fiction—and I created dishes to share. Dishes with corny names and inside jokes, from imaginary realms made with mythical ingredients. Then I went to the grocery store and figured out how to create these ideas in the real world. I hope you like it and that you share it with all your super-fan friends (preferably in costume).

Leslie Bilderback

Magical Menus

WIZARD'S SUMMER PICNIC

Lusty Month of May Potato Soup 32
Emerald Lobster Rice Salad 180
Gandalf's Cold Chicken and Pickles 70
Butterfly Cake 150
Butterbeer 96

PLANNING AHEAD

Chilled Lusty Month of May Potato Soup:
Make the soup a day ahead, chill overnight,
and then pack in a thermos.
Butterfly Cake:
Bake the cake in cupcake form.

SET THE SCENE

Buy star-studded fabric to use as a picnic blanket;
and offer a magic-wand craft activity, foraging
sticks on site, and wrapping the ends with colorful
yarns for a wizard's grip.

EXOTIC WITCHES' & WARLOCKS' DINNER

Cornish Pasties, Savory Pumpkin Filling 94
Witches' Brew, Coconut Shrimp Green Curry 54
Dr. Bombay's Chicken Tikka Masala 194
Bundt Friday Cake with Truth Sprinkles 200

PLANNING AHEAD

Cornish Pasties, Savory Pumpkin Filling:
Toss 2 tablespoons freshly grated ginger into the
pumpkin filling to keep the Asian flavor theme.
Bundt Friday Cake with Truth Sprinkles:
Add 2 tablespoons Chinese Five Spice to batter
with the flour, garnish with black sesame seeds and
candied ginger.

SET THE SCENE

Make a table runner with slightly shredded
cheesecloth dyed in strong tea and a centerpiece
using moss, greens, black feathers, bare branches
painted black, and various candles.

ARABIAN NIGHTS SUPPER CLUB

Minted Arak Tea, recipe below
Roasted Chickpeas, recipe below
Jinni's Careless Pistachio Goat Cheese Dates 36
Ghūl-ish Kebabs 40
Jasmine Rice
Hummus with Grilled Pita Bread
Sliced Garden Tomatoes
Lemon Wedges
Arabic Coffee and Cardamom Cookies 38
Arabic Coffee, see below

PLANNING AHEAD

Minted Arak Tea:
Mix 6 cups iced mint tea, 4 ounces arak, 1 teaspoon
orange flower or rose water, and 2 tablespoons
sugar. Serve over ice and garnish with mint leaves.
Roasted Chickpeas:
Spread canned chickpeas on a baking sheet; roast
at 375°F for 30-45 minutes, stirring occasionally,
until dry and crisp. Transfer to a bowl, toss with olive oil
and 7 Spice mix. Cool, and serve with cocktails.
Arabic Coffee:
Brew your favorite dark roast (or decaf)
with a teaspoon of cardamom added to the filter.

SET THE SCENE

Use a gold table runner, and table linens in assorted
jewel tones. Use brass or golden tableware and
containers to hold flowers of assorted jewel tones,
while scattering multicolored plastic gems.

ENCHANTED DISNEY DINNER

Dumbo's Pink Elephant Punch, recipe below
The Gray Stuff 170
Baguettes
Aladdin's Magical Garden Salad 42
We Are Not a Codfish and Chips 138
Elsa's Raspberry Snow Queens 156

PLANNING AHEAD

Dumbo's Pink Elephant Punch:
In a large pitcher or punch bowl with ice, combine
1 bottle pink champagne, 1 cup vodka, ½ cup
Grand Marnier, and 1 pint sliced strawberries.
Serve in fluted glasses.

SET THE SCENE

Use black, white, and primary colored table linens.
Make a Mickey centerpiece by spray painting black
one large and two small Styrofoam balls. Secure into
a Mickey shape with hot glue, insert a black dowel into
the neck, add a red ribbon bow tie, and insert into floral
arrangement of red flowers. Make a second Minnie
head by adding a red polka dot hair bow.

STAR WARS
THAT'S NO MOON DINNER

Kyber Crystal Cocktails 108
Cantina Cocktail Snack Mix 116
Canto Bight Clams Casino 120
Alderaan Gorak Roasted in Malla Petals 118
Quinoa-Jin and Cuke Skywalker Salad,
recipe below
Blue Milk Pudding 122

PLANNING AHEAD

Quinoa-Jin and Cuke Skywalker Salad:
Cook quinoa as directed, cool to room temperature,
chill. Toss together sliced cucumber, thinly sliced red
onion, halved cherry tomato, and fresh oregano.
Dress with your favorite vinaigrette.
Just before serving, toss in chilled quinoa.

SET THE SCENE

Use black and dark-blue table linens with silver and
black tableware. Use round vases or fishbowls to
create planet-shaped floral arrangements by filling
with green glass stones and green-hued flowers.
Scatter green or silver sequin stars.

HALLOWEEN COCKTAIL PARTY

- Crystal Ball Cocktails 228
- Salem's Black Cat Cocktail 202
- Salem's Flying Ointment (Chicken Rillettes) 238
- Assorted Crackers
- Toad in the Hole 140
- Glamorgan Sausages 28
- Sleepy Hollow Silverside of Beef Sliders 234
- Assorted Crudités with Cauldron Dip, recipe below
- Rhubarb Pickles in Port 52
- Eclipse Cookies 30

PLANNING AHEAD

Toad in the Hole:
Bake in small muffin tins.

Glamorgan Sausages:
Form into bite-size balls for cocktail-sized nibbling.

Sleepy Hollow Silverside of Beef Sliders:
Serve on Bread of the Dead rolls (86) with curried mayonnaise and onion.

Cauldron Dip:
In a blender, combine 1 cup ricotta, 2 cups frozen (defrosted) edamame or green peas, ½ cup prepared pesto, juice of 1 lemon, and a pinch of salt. Blend. Add olive oil until desired consistency for dipping is reached. Serve in a cauldron (obviously), sprinkled with poppy or black sesame seeds.

Eclipse Cookies:
Frost in a crescent-moon design.

SET THE SCENE

Use all white or all black table linens. Hollow out white pumpkins to use as flower vases and fill with dried leaves and twigs painted black. Place skulls and bones throughout, with lots of black candles.

A MAGICAL RENAISSANCE MEAL

- Turmeric Tincture Cocktail, recipe below
- Caliban's Hot Crab Dip 58
- Crusaders Saffron Lamb with Lemon 24
- Thistle Salad 80
- Lemon Mercury Torte 220
- Mulled Wine

PLANNING AHEAD

Caliban's Hot Crab Dip:
Leave off the tropical salsa for a more accurate Renaissance experience.

Turmeric Tincture Cocktail:
Mix 2 ounces rum, the juice and zest of ½ lime, and 1 teaspoon Nicolas Flamel's Elixirs of Life (page 218). Serve over ice with fresh cilantro or mint leaves, topped with seltzer or ginger ale.

SET THE SCENE

Use burlap as a table runner with dark burgundy or brown table linens. Use bows of raw twine as napkin rings and tuck in assorted sprigs of fresh herbs. Use bowls of fresh fruit—such as oranges, apples, and grapes—as a centerpiece, with assorted fresh herbs tucked in between, and lots of low candles.

1

The Arthurian Legend

Today, tales of Merlin and King Arthur are known mainly from film and television. But they originated in ancient Welsh literature, shared first in the oral tradition of folklore and written down as early as the eighth century. The figure of Merlin did not start off as the magical sorcerer we think of today. He is first described as a prophet-advisor, tutor to four successive kings of Britain, the last Celtic shaman, and keeper of the Druids' ancient secrets. The son of a nun and an incubus, Merlin had the potential for both holiness and wickedness. These are the characteristics that were later built upon by various authors—and Hollywood directors.

Queen Ganieda's Apple Pork Pie

Serves 8-10

Geoffrey of Monmouth, a Welsh cleric, is best known for *Historia Regum Britanniae (The History of the Kings of Britain)*. He popularized the idea of King Arthur, who at fifteen became king of Britain. "Vita Merlini" ("The Life of Merlin"), from the middle twelfth century, is Monmouth's account of Merlin. Ruler of the kingdom of Dyfed, Merlin went insane at the sight of loved ones slain in battle. He ran off to live in the enchanted Caledonian Forest, where he spoke to the animals and found protection in magical apple trees.

His sister, Ganieda, queen of the Cumbrians, brought Merlin back to courtly life, but he claimed he could see the future and was considered mad. As a test, she brought him three boys and asked how each would die. The boys, however, were the same boy in different disguises. Merlin gave three answers—dies in a fall, dies in a tree, dies in a river. Ganieda proclaimed he could not see the future. Years later, the boy fell from a cliff, got caught in a tree, and dangled headfirst in a river, where he drowned. Merlin's madness was eventually cured by water from a magical spring. He prophesied the invasion of Britain by the Normans and lived out his days in the woods, where Ganieda eventually joined him.

Medieval meat pies were more of a preservation method than a culinary creation. Meat, cooked and preserved in fat (the natural jelly that occurs from the concentration of juices) and a dense crust, kept the meat edible longer. In fact, the crust was often discarded. You'll want to eat this crust though, because it is flaky and delicious.

PIE DOUGH

This recipe is suitable for both sweet and savory pies.

3 cups all-purpose flour
1 tablespoon sugar
1 teaspoon sea salt
¼-½ cup ice water
1 teaspoon apple cider vinegar or lemon juice
1 cup (2 sticks, 8 ounces) cold unsalted butter, cubed
(for a more authentically medieval dough, use lard)

1. In a large bowl, combine flour, sugar, and salt. Combine ice water and vinegar in another bowl. Using a fork or fingers, cut the butter into the flour mixture until it resembles a coarse meal. Make a well in the center, add ¼ cup of the ice water mix, and mix with a fork until a dry dough forms. (Add more water if necessary, but do not allow the dough to become wet.)

2. Turn the dough out onto a floured surface and knead briefly until it holds together. Press it into a disk about 1-inch thick, wrap in plastic, and refrigerate for at least 30 minutes, up to 24 hours. Longer storage of dough should be done in the freezer.

Queen Janieda's Apple Pork Pie (continued)

PIE FILLING

4 slices bacon
1 pound ground pork
1 pound pork butt or shoulder, cubed
2 tablespoons olive oil
1 yellow onion, diced
1 stalk celery, diced
3 cloves garlic
2 apples, peeled, cored, and sliced
2 cups chicken broth
1 teaspoon sea salt
¼ teaspoon ground clove
½ teaspoon freshly grated nutmeg
¼ teaspoon ground allspice
1 recipe Pie Dough
2 large eggs, divided
1 cup chopped Italian parsley
1 tablespoon water

1. Cook bacon in a large heavy skillet over high heat until fat is melted and meat is crispy. Add ground pork and pork butt. Cook, stirring, for 5 to 10 minutes, until well browned, and cooked through. Remove from skillet and set aside.

2. Add oil to the skillet, and return to heat. Add onion and celery and cook over high heat until translucent. Add garlic and continue cooking until golden. Add back the meat, along with apples, broth, salt, and spices. Cook, stirring occasionally, until the liquid has evaporated, about 30 minutes. Remove from heat, transfer to a bowl, and cool to room temperature. (This can be done a day ahead and kept in the refrigerator.)

3. Coat a 9-inch pie pan with nonstick spray. Dust work surface with flour, pinching off only as much dough as you'll need for one 9-inch circle (about half the recipe). Knead briefly to soften slightly, pat into a disk, and roll out a circle a couple of inches larger than your pan, no more than ¼-inch thick. (For best results, roll in one direction only, giving the dough a quarter turn after each roll. Roll, turn, roll, turn, until it's the size you need. This way, you'll keep it roundish and will know instantly if it starts to stick, enabling you to compensate with a dusting of flour.) Line the pie pan, pressing the dough into place. Roll a second, slightly larger disk. Set aside in refrigerator.

4. Add 1 egg and parsley into the cooled meat mixture and mix thoroughly. Transfer to the pie pan, mound it up, and smooth the top. Place the second pie dough circle on top. Pinch the edges of the top and bottom dough together, and trim to a ½-inch overhang. Crimp the edges decoratively, and freeze until the dough is solid, about 30 minutes. Preheat oven to 350°F.

5. Whisk remaining egg with water and brush top of pie. Slice a few decorative vents in the top, and bake for about an hour, until the crust is golden brown and the filling is bubbly. Cool and serve warm, at room temperature, or chilled with mustard and pickles.

VARIATION
Try other fruits. Pears and dried fruits are a natural, as are cranberries and pomegranate seeds.

French Medieval Poached Pears

Serves 4-8

Chrétien de Troyes was a twelfth-century French poet, who likely served the court of Marie de France, Countess of Champagne, in the 1160s, during which he began five Arthurian romance poems. Courtly romances were popular, and de Troyes took advantage of their popularity by incorporating elements and characters of the Arthur story, including Gawain, Guinevere (Arthur's wife), and especially Lancelot.

"Erec and Enide," the first of de Troyes's five romance poems, is of Guinevere's knight Erec and his love affair with Enide. "Lancelot, the Knight of the Cart" is the first story to feature a love affair between Arthur's wife and his best friend. "Yvain, the Knight of the Lion" is about a knight who must win back the love of his lady. He is faced with a menacing Black Knight, giants, demons, and a magical storm-making stone, but succeeds with the help of a lion he rescues from a dragon. "Cligès" tells the tale of a knight's love for his uncle's wife. De Troyes also penned "Perceval," the story of a quest for a grail, left unfinished at his death, but completed by others. It does not refer to the grail as holy and makes no connection to Christianity—this will come later with Robert de Boron.

In the medieval period, certain fruit was fit only for nobility and often served at the end of a meal. Tree fruit, especially, was thought to be earth's most noble produce. This is because fruit that grew in trees was closer to heaven. Medieval doctors considered fruit to be of no nutritional value, and in some cases, detrimental to health. But because the courtiers loved it, doctors prescribed it to be consumed only in a cooked state. Apples, pears, and nuts were thought useful in pushing food down toward its outlet, and confined to the end of a meal. Pears, considered the hardest to digest, were always cooked in wine and spices.

3 cups sweet white wine
(Sauternes, Riesling,
or Gewürztraminer)
4 tablespoons butter
1 tablespoon sugar
2 or 3 strips of orange zest
3 or 4 cloves
1 roughly crushed cinnamon stick
Pinch sea salt
4 pears
1-2 cups water
1 cup sliced, toasted almonds

1. Combine wine, butter, sugar, orange zest, cloves, cinnamon, and salt in a large pot. Place over high heat. Peel pears, but leave whole, and add to the liquid. Add enough water to cover the pears and bring to a boil. At the boil, reduce the heat to a simmer and cover. Cook for 20 to 30 minutes, or until the pears are tender.

2. Remove the pears from the liquid and set aside to cool. Increase the heat once again, and reduce the liquid to sauce consistency. Strain and set aside to serve with the pears.

3. Halve the cooled pears and remove the core with a melon baller. Serve pear halves with a drizzle of sauce and a sprinkle of sliced almonds.

Robert de Boron, "Merlin"

Crusaders Saffron Lamb with Preserved Lemon

Serves 6-8

In the late twelfth century, Robert de Boron reworked the Merlin story into Old French as part of a trilogy revolving around the Holy Grail. The trilogy, "Joseph of Arimathea," "Perceval," and "Merlin," were the first to link the Arthurian legend with Christianity, where it remains to this day. From it, we find the origins of the stories we know, including Merlin's role as the prophet assistant to King Pendragon, the birth of Arthur, the sword in the stone (originally the sword was stuck in an anvil atop a stone), and the chivalrous aspects of the Round Table, derived from the burial of British soldiers at Stonehenge (which is round) after a battle with Saxon invaders. It is here that the quest for the Holy Grail became the central theme, and the one task from which a knight may prove his worthiness.

In the eleventh century, an attempt was made to help Eastern Christians of the Byzantine Empire who were under Muslim attack. But rather than return captured territory to the Byzantines, territories were divided amongst European crusaders. What followed was a centuries-long battle. There were nine Crusades in all, spanning nearly 200 years, ostensibly carried out to make pilgrimage to sacred sites safe for Europeans. The idea of the Crusade continued well into the fifteenth century, though the focus shifted to the acquisition of territory and the New World. It was with Robert de Boron's help that Western culture felt it somehow had moral authority. One effect of the Crusades was the introduction to the West of exotic goods from the East. Pillaged wares, including textiles, metalwork, and spices, were returned to Europe and became fashionable in the elite circles of the European courts.

4 tablespoons olive oil
1 teaspoon saffron threads
1 rack of lamb
2 cloves garlic
Grated zest and juice of 1 lemon
1 teaspoon sea salt
1 teaspoon cracked black pepper
2 cups fresh Italian parsley leaves
¼ cup diced preserved lemon
2 white onions, sliced
1 cup plain yogurt

1. Warm the oil in a small pan over low heat or in a microwave for 30 seconds, until it is just too hot to touch. Crumble in saffron threads and steep in the warmed oil for 10 to 15 minutes. Meanwhile, pierce the lamb rack all over with a sharp paring knife.

2. In a food processor, combine garlic, lemon zest and juice, salt, pepper, parsley, and preserved lemon. Pulse to a puree, then slowly add saffron oil and process into a paste. Rub all but ¼ cup of the saffron herb paste over the lamb. Place in a zipper bag, and refrigerate to marinate for 12 to 24 hours. (The longer the marinating time, the better the flavor.)

3. Preheat oven to 450°F. Line a roasting pan with sliced onions, and place the lamb on top. Roast for 15 minutes at 450°F, then reduce oven to 350°F. Continue roasting for 20 to 30 minutes, or to desired doneness. (Check internal temperature: medium-rare is 145°F.) Remove from the oven, cover, and rest 10 minutes before slicing into chops between ribs. Stir reserved saffron herb paste into the yogurt and serve a dollop alongside the sliced lamb.

VARIATION
You can make this on a much larger scale, too. Rather than a rack, make it with a whole lamb leg. Roasting time will increase during the 350°F section to 1½ hours.

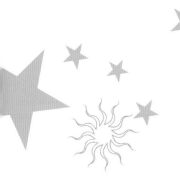

Royal Christmastide Pottage

Serves 6-8

A heroic figure from the earliest known Welsh tales, Sir Gawain appears in several Knights of the Round Table stories. He is best known as the hero of "Sir Gawain and the Green Knight," a mid-fourteenth-century chivalric romance written by an unknown author. It is set during a Christmas (or New Year's) feast and, like all medieval literature, gives an interesting view into what life was like in the royal court.

As the meal begins, a strange knight appears in the banquet hall to test the honor of the Round Table. He is dressed head to toe in green, has green skin and a green beard, and is riding a green horse with red eyes. His challenge is to allow Arthur to strike him down with a single blow of an ax on the condition that he must accept the consequences of a return blow in exactly one year. Arthur agrees, but is interrupted by his nephew, Sir Gawain, who accepts the challenge on the king's behalf, lest the king be put in peril.

Gawain beheads the Green Knight with one blow, but the knight picks up his own head, repeats the terms of the agreement, and then rides away. A year later, Gawain sets out to fulfill his promise to the Green Knight. What follows is a tale of chivalric code, bargains, honor, and the power of a woman's attention.

A pottage is simply something that has been cooked in a pot. The texture can vary from stewy to soupy, and it is made with an infinite variety of ingredients. At Christmastime, however, a pottage is made with the most precious ingredients, often preserved all year for this sacred celebration.

3 tablespoons unsalted butter
2 pounds beef shanks
2 cups red wine
1 bottle stout
½ cup dried currants
½ cup golden raisins
½ cup dried figs, quartered
½ cup pitted dates, quartered
1 pinch ground clove
½ teaspoon freshly grated nutmeg
2 apples (Fuji or other mildly tart apple), peeled and diced
1 teaspoon sea salt
1 teaspoon black pepper

1. In a large, heavy stew pot, melt butter over medium-high heat. Add beef shanks and brown on all sides. Do not crowd—this may need to be done in batches. When all the beef is brown, add it all to the pot, add wine and stout, and bring to a boil. At the boil, reduce heat to a bare simmer, and cover. Cook for 1 hour.

2. At the 1-hour mark, add the dried fruits and spices. Cover and continue simmering for another hour. Add water to the pot if necessary to keep the meat covered.

3. At the end of the second hour, add apples and continue cooking until they are tender, but still chunky, about 20 minutes. Remove the meat, cool slightly, and separate it from the bone. Chop or shred meat to bite-size pieces and return to the pot. Season with salt and pepper. Serve in deep bowls with crusty pieces of bread.

VARIATION
A variety of meats can be used in place of the beef, but wild, gamey meats are more authentic. Try it with venison, boar, lamb, or goat. Turkey and goose would be excellent substitutes as well.

Glamorgan Sausages

Makes 10

Thomas Malory was a thirteenth-century gentleman and knight embroiled in the Wars of the Roses—a battle for the throne of England between the two noble dynasties of York and Lancaster. Malory was imprisoned for a series of violent crimes likely associated with this conflict. He called himself the knight prisoner, and it was while imprisoned that he penned tales of Arthur, Guinevere, the quest for the Holy Grail, and the love between Guinevere and Lancelot. There are twenty-one chapters (or books) in *Le Morte d'Arthur* that take readers from the founding of the kingdom to Arthur's death and the kingdom's fall. Malory concentrates his themes on the brotherhood of the knights.

Glamorgan is a Welsh region along the river Usk, named after an Arthurian court. It appears in *Le Morte d'Arthur* as a property given by Arthur to Sir Gawain after winning a duel against Galleron of Galloway. Glamorgan sausage is sausage in name only, more of a vegetarian cheese fritter in a sausage shape. The original recipe may have included meat, but this version became popular during the World Wars when meat was scarce. Early recipes show addition of cloves, sage, or ginger (very medieval indeed). This is a more modern version still served in the region. It is traditionally made with Caerphilly, a soft, white, crumbly Welsh cow's milk cheese. If you cannot find Caerphilly, the recipe works equally well with other cheeses. Try a combination of Jack, Cheddar, and Muenster or Havarti in equal parts.

1 tablespoon unsalted butter
1 leek, chopped
1 tablespoon fresh chopped thyme
1½ cups crumbled Caerphilly cheese
2 cups breadcrumbs, divided
2 eggs, divided
2 tablespoons milk
1 tablespoon Dijon mustard
1 teaspoon sea salt
½ teaspoon black pepper
¼ cup all-purpose flour
2-3 cups vegetable oil for frying

1. Melt butter in a large, heavy skillet over medium heat. Add leek and thyme and cook, stirring, until golden brown, about 5 minutes.

2. Combine leeks in a large bowl with cheese, 1 cup of the breadcrumbs, 1 egg, milk, mustard, salt, and pepper. Mix thoroughly, divide into 10 portions, and form into sausage shapes.

3. Combine remaining breadcrumbs with flour. Beat remaining egg. Coat each sausage with flour, then egg, then flour again. Set aside at room temperature.

4. Fill a heavy skillet with about 1 inch of oil and heat to 375°F (a crumb tossed in should sizzle immediately). Cook sausages in batches, turning until evenly browned, about 3 to 5 minutes. Drain off excess oil on paper towels. Season with salt. Serve with mustard, pickles, and beer.

Mark Twain, *A Connecticut Yankee in King Arthur's Court*

Eclipse Cookies

Makes about 1 dozen

First published in 1889, this tale by Mark Twain tells of a nineteenth-century man sent back to King Arthur's court via a bump on the head. The Yankee, named Hank Morgan, uses his knowledge of nineteenth-century technology to present himself as a powerful magician, surpassing the power and influence of Merlin. His initial trick occurs at the moment of his execution, when, with foreknowledge of an eclipse, he threatens to block out the sun if not released. With that, Morgan becomes a trusted advisor to the king, and the nemesis of Merlin. He constructs a nineteenth-century infrastructure, teaches his modern ideas to the youth, and eventually falls in love, marries, and has a family.

Twain took material from Thomas Malory, adding satirical themes mocking medieval feudalism, the monarchy, and courtly life. The story championed industrialization and democracy and criticized slavery, taxation, and the power of the church—issues very much on the mind of his nineteenth-century audience. Though it is a comedy, there are several disturbing scenes in which a knight's lance is no match for Hank's modern weaponry.

A proper black-and-white cookie is more cake than cookie, similar to a proper French madeleine but much larger and frosted. They are a New York tradition, so the best way to know if you've made them correctly is to invite a New Yorker over for a taste test.

COOKIES

Grated zest of 1 lemon
½ cup granulated sugar
1/3 cup unsalted butter, at room temperature
1 large egg
1¼ cups all-purpose flour
½ teaspoon baking soda
½ teaspoon sea salt
1/3 cup buttermilk
½ teaspoon vanilla extract

FROSTING

1½ cups powdered sugar
1 tablespoon corn syrup
1 tablespoon lemon juice
1 teaspoon vanilla extract
1 tablespoon water
¼ cup cocoa powder

1. Preheat oven to 350°F. Line a baking sheet with parchment paper. Combine lemon zest and sugar in a food processor. Pulse until the sugar is yellow and fragrant.

2. In a stand mixer or bowl with a hand mixer, beat together butter and lemon-sugar until smooth and lump free. Add egg and incorporate fully.

3. In a separate bowl, combine flour, baking soda, and salt. Add to batter alternating with the buttermilk and vanilla in three increments.

4. Using a 2-3-ounce ice cream scoop, scoop dough and arrange on prepared baking sheet about 2 inches apart. (They can be made in any size—larger will need to cook a little longer, smaller a little less.) Bake until golden brown, about 15 minutes. Cool completely.

5. For icing, in a medium bowl, combine powdered sugar, corn syrup, lemon juice, and vanilla. Mix until smooth. Add water as needed until the frosting is thin but spreadable. Remove half to a separate bowl, add cocoa powder and stir, and then enough additional water to match the white frosting consistency.

6. Working on the flat side of each cookie, spread half with chocolate icing and half with vanilla icing. Do not stack them, unless they are individually wrapped.

Lusty Month of May Potato Soup

Serves 6-8

Between 1938 and 1941, British author T. H. White wrote stories based on the work of Thomas Malory: *The Sword in the Stone*, *The Queen of Air and Darkness*, *The Ill-Made Knight*, and *The Candle in the Wind*. In 1958, these stories were revised, amended, and compiled under the title *The Once and Future King*. This is of note because among other things, parts were adapted into well-known plays and films. Walt Disney bought the rights to *The Sword in the Stone* and forever ingrained the idea of Merlin as a bumbling wizard, living backward in time, teaching young Arthur how to be a good king by turning him into animals. Alan Jay Lerner and Frederick Loewe based their play *Camelot* on *The Ill-Made Knight* and *The Candle in the Wind*. Its first Broadway production won four Tony Awards in 1960 and was produced as a film in 1967.

May Day is likely a holdover from the Roman festival of Flora, the goddess of flowers and spring. Such festivities, mentioned by the poet Ovid, celebrated spring, new growth, and birth. Symbols such as the maypole, wreaths, and garlands have been used for "bringing in the May" since the fourteenth century. Though fertility rites were probably not practiced in medieval times, they were alluded to with feasting, drinking, gaming, music, and dancing. This was frowned on by sixteenth-century Puritans, as gluttony and lust were considered sins. In Lerner and Loewe's *Camelot*, it is at the May Day festival where Arthur introduces Lancelot to Guinevere—an event with its own lustful consequences.

2 tablespoons olive oil
½ cup chopped pancetta or ham
3 cups chopped green garlic (also known as spring garlic), divided
5 cups white new or fingerling potatoes, quartered
2-3 cups vegetable or chicken broth
1 teaspoon sea salt
¼ teaspoon ground white pepper
¼ teaspoon freshly grated nutmeg
½ cup cream
1 tablespoon sesame seeds

1. Heat oil in a heavy-bottomed soup pot. Add pancetta and cook until crispy. Add 2¼ cups of the garlic. Continue cooking until just tender. Add potatoes, broth, salt, pepper, and nutmeg. Bring to a boil. At the boil, reduce heat to a simmer. Continue cooking until potatoes are tender, about 30 minutes.

2. Remove the potatoes from the pot. Puree them with an immersion blender or in a blender, working in batches of potatoes with a little cooking liquid.

3. Add the potatoes back to the pot. Reheat. Add the cream. Season with salt as needed and garnish with remaining chopped green garlic and sesame seeds.

VARIATION
This makes a great vichyssoise. Serve it well chilled, preferably in an icer (a soup dish nestled in crushed ice).

2
1001 Arabian Nights

Arabian Nights is a compilation of Middle Eastern folklore from the Islamic Golden Age spanning the eighth to fourteenth centuries, an unparalleled period of cultural achievement. Baghdad, established in 762 CE, was the seat of the Abbasid Caliphate. There, the caliphs created a space for knowledge known as the House of Wisdom. Scholars were recruited from around the world to share ideas. They translated all the Greek works into Arabic and assimilated ideas on medicine, philosophy, astronomy, and economics. They acquired papermaking and printing technology from China and turned their achievements into books long before Gutenberg. It all ended, however, in 1258, with the Mongol invasion, the siege of Baghdad, and the collapse of the Abbasid Caliphate.

Arabian Nights is also an international compilation, including tales from cultures across Africa and Asia. They are framed under a single premise, which probably originated in Persia. The ruler Shahryār discovers his wife has been unfaithful, so he vows to marry a virgin each night, and then kill her in the morning, never giving her a chance to be unfaithful. Eventually, the only maiden left is Scheherazade, the daughter of the vizier. In order to prolong her life, and keep the king perpetually in need of her, Scheherazade entertains him with stories. Cleverly, she prolongs their climax until the morning, when the entertainments must stop, guaranteeing her one more night to finish the story. The number of her tales has varied throughout the ages, from 100 to beyond the 1,001. Some of the stories are framed within other tales, while some begin and end on their own. Interestingly, the most recognizable tales to Westerners–"Aladdin," "Sinbad," and "Ali Baba and the Forty Thieves"— were not part of the Arabic original, but added by the French translator Antoine Galland in the late seventeenth century, who claimed to have heard them from a Syrian passing through Paris. The first English translation of the tales was printed in 1706 and included the Frenchman's additions.

"The Tale of the Trader and the Jinni"

Jinni's Careless Dates

Dating from the pre-Islamic era, jinn are spirits that haunt the Arabian Desert. Their bodies are made of fire, but they can shape-shift. They can be mischievous or mean, but will sometimes grant wishes. In "The Tale of the Trader and the Jinni," a merchant stops for a snack then tosses his date pits. An angry jinni appears, revealing that a pit has struck and killed his son. The jinni intends to kill the merchant but is convinced to wait a year, giving the merchant a chance to say goodbye to his own family. Upon his return a year later, three old men meet the merchant, each accompanied by an animal. When the jinni arrives, the old men distract him with stories of their animals, which are actually enchanted family members. These stories convince the jinni to spare the merchant.

Dates have an important legacy in the ancient world. Besides being eaten as is, they were used for making both wine and sugar. Their sweetness is the perfect platform for all sorts of flavors, and it's hard to pick just one. So don't bother. Here are five delicious variations on the stuffed date. I prefer juicy Medjool dates for stuffing because they're soft and large enough for a couple bites. You can use any date you prefer—just make sure they are tender. Remove the pits from the center by tearing them open lengthwise along one side, which creates a pocket.

PARMESAN DATES
Makes 2 dozen

2-ounce block good-quality
Parmesan cheese (Reggiano)
2 dozen dates, pits removed

1. Peel off slices of Parmesan with a potato peeler. Insert two or three 1-inch pieces into each date's pocket. Pinch closed. Serve at room temperature to bring out the cheese's flavor.

BACON PECAN DATES
Makes 1 dozen

12 pecan halves
1 dozen dates, pits removed
5-6 slices bacon, cooked and
crumbled

1. Preheat oven to 350°F. Spread the pecans out onto a dry baking sheet and bake for 10 to 15 minutes, or until fragrant and toasted. Cool.

2. Fill each date cavity with a generous pinch of crumbled bacon, then a toasted pecan half. Pinch closed. Warm in the oven for 5 minutes before serving.

PISTACHIO
GOAT CHEESE DATES
Makes 1 dozen

1 cup goat cheese
1 tablespoon honey
1 tablespoon rose water
Pinch sea salt
1 dozen dates, pits removed
1 cup finely chopped pistachios

1. In a bowl, stir together cheese, honey, rose water, and salt. Transfer to a piping bag, and use it to fill each date cavity.

2. Spread the pistachios out onto a plate and dip the cheese side of each date in them, coating the cheese that is visible with chopped nuts. Serve chilled or at room temperature.

COCONUT WALNUT DATES
Makes 1 dozen

1 cup walnuts
1 cup unsweetened coconut
½ teaspoon freshly cracked
black pepper
1 dozen dates, pits removed

1. Preheat oven to 350°F. Spread the walnuts out onto a dry baking sheet and bake for 10 to 15 minutes, or until fragrant and toasted. Cool slightly.

2. Transfer walnuts to a food processor. Pulse until very fine. Add coconut and pepper. Grind to a paste consistency. With a small spoon, fill each date's cavity, then pinch it closed.

CHOCOLATE
PEANUT BUTTER DATES
Makes 1 dozen

These dates are stuffed with a variation on ganache. It's super easy and versatile. Once you master it (which doesn't take long), it can be used for truffles, tart fillings, frosting or glaze for cakes, or chocolate sauce.

4 ounces bittersweet chocolate
2 tablespoons smooth peanut butter
½ teaspoon sea salt, divided
¼ cup heavy cream
1 dozen dates, pits removed

1. Chop chocolate into small pieces. Place in a bowl with the peanut butter and half the salt.

2. Warm the cream in a small saucepan over medium-high heat. As soon as it starts to boil, remove it from the heat, and pour it over the chocolate bowl. Shake the bowl so that that all the chocolate is submerged, then set aside, untouched, for 5 minutes.

3. At the 5-minute mark, whisk smooth, then set aside at room temperature to harden, about 1 hour. (Don't refrigerate or it will get too hard to pipe.)

4. Transfer to a piping bag. Fill the cavity of each date. Sprinkle the remaining sea salt on top of the dates. Serve chilled or at room temperature.

Arabic Coffee and Cardamom Cookies

Makes about 2 dozen

By the time the king met Scheherazade, he had murdered 1,001 wives. Despite her father's objections, she volunteered to spend one night with him. Scheherazade was a great storyteller, having been well educated in history, science, philosophy, and poetry. The king agreed and was entranced. But Scheherazade stopped halfway through, because it was dawn and her time to die. The king granted her one more night to finish her story. The next night, after the first tale ended, she began another, and the cycle repeated. After 1,001 nights, Scheherazade revealed that she was out of stories. But by that time, the king had fallen madly in love with her, and so the two were married.

Cardamom is a beloved spice worldwide. In India, it's used in curry. In Scandinavia, it's used in pastry. In the Arabic world, it's added to coffee. If you are skeptical, this recipe will help you understand just how terrific that coffee is.

½ cup skin-on almonds, chopped
1 cup (2 sticks, 8 ounces), unsalted butter, softened
1 cup granulated sugar, plus extra for garnish
1 cup dark brown sugar
¼ cup instant espresso or coffee
1 tablespoon ground cardamom
1 teaspoon sea salt
2 large eggs
1 teaspoon vanilla extract
1 teaspoon baking powder
2¾ cups all-purpose flour
½ cup cocoa nibs

1. Preheat oven to 350°F. Spread out the chopped almonds onto a dry baking sheet and bake for 10 to 15 minutes, until fragrant and toasted. Cool completely.

2. In a large bowl, cream together butter, both sugars, espresso, cardamom, and salt until smooth and lump free. Add eggs one at a time, then the vanilla, stirring to incorporate thoroughly. Slowly add baking powder, then the flour in two or three increments. Fold in cocoa nibs and cooled almonds.

3. Using an ice cream scoop (or two spoons) drop walnut-size balls of dough onto a baking sheet, 1 inch apart. Sprinkle each cookie with a pinch of granulated sugar, then bake for 12 to 18 minutes, until firm. Cool completely and store in an airtight container.

VARIATIONS
Rose Water and Saffron: Use all granulated sugar (replace brown sugar with equal amount of granulated). Combine 2 tablespoons of white sugar with 3 or 4 threads of saffron. Pulse together in a coffee mill or crush in a mortar. Add this with the regular sugar as directed. Replace the vanilla with an equal amount of rose water. Omit the instant espresso and cocoa nibs.

Chocolate Cardamom: Replace ½ cup of flour with an equal amount of cocoa powder, and omit the instant espresso. Replace almonds with 1 cup of chocolate chunks.

Ghũl-ish Kebabs

Serves 4-6

The source of the English word *ghouls*, ghũls are creatures from pre-Islamic Bedouin poetry that roam cemeteries and the desert wilderness at night. They are always evil and enjoy eating humans. They are a subclass of jinn that can be recognized because they have ass hooves. They are known to distract travelers by assuming pleasing shapes, usually attractive women. They then lure the travelers into the wilderness. Ghũls can be killed, but only by one blow. If you take another swing, they will come back to life.

There are dozens of kebab variations throughout the Middle East. But sometimes, simple is better. This recipe is easy but contains the essential flavors of sumac, 7-spice mix, cilantro, and lemon that make it taste exotic.

2-3 pounds flank steak
1 tablespoon ground sumac
1 tablespoon ground cumin
1 tablespoon Lebanese 7-Spice Mix (recipe follows)
1 teaspoon sea salt
1 cup chopped cilantro, plus extra for garnish
4 cloves garlic, minced
Grated zest and juice of 1 lemon
Olive oil for serving

1. Slice meat across the grain into 1- to 2-inch strips. Place in a zip-top bag and add sumac, cumin, 7-spice mix, salt, cilantro, garlic, and lemon zest and juice. Zip the bag, massage the meat to distribute flavors, then refrigerate to marinate for 6 hours, or overnight.

2. Preheat grill on high heat. Thread marinated beef strips onto metal kebab skewers, pleating the meat as you go. Don't pack too tightly. Brush lightly with olive oil, then grill for 5 minutes on each side, or to desired doneness. Serve over rice with a drizzle of olive oil, flat bread, a generous pinch of cilantro, and wedges of lemon.

LEBANESE 7-SPICE MIX

If possible, grind these spices fresh from whole seeds.
¼ cup black pepper
¼ cup ground cumin
¼ cup paprika
2 tablespoons ground coriander
2 tablespoons ground clove
2 teaspoons ground nutmeg
2 teaspoons ground cinnamon

1. Combine spices and store in an airtight container.

"Aladdin"

Aladdin's Magical Garden Salad

Serves 4-6

The story "Aladdin" is a European addition that begins with a description of the boy in China, a common European story form of the seventeenth and eighteenth centuries. (Europeans were fascinated by everything exotic.) The story is entirely set in China. That we know it today as an Arabic tale is a fascinating mutation.

Many other elements have also disappeared. Aladdin's mother, embarrassed by her son's laziness, played a role in the original story. He was chosen by an African magician who pretended to be his uncle, but really needed a foolish lad to find a magic lamp. There is a long journey, a magic ring that can conjure a jinni, and a magical garden of fruit trees through which Aladdin must pass to retrieve a magic lamp. There's a jinni in the lamp and a princess that Aladdin eventually weds. The jinni also tricks Aladdin to get out of the lamp, but they still live happily ever after.

This refreshing salad features the usual combination of sweet and salty fruits and vegetables to create Aladdin-worthy flavors of wonder. The ingredient za'atar is a staple pantry ingredient in the Arabic world. Though the blend varies regionally, it typically includes an herb (such as thyme or oregano), sesame seeds, and sumac.

½ red onion, sliced
1 cup crumbled feta cheese
1 cup mayonnaise
1 teaspoon honey
1 teaspoon sea salt
½ teaspoon black pepper
1 teaspoon za'atar
1 cup fresh or frozen (and defrosted) peas
1 Persian cucumber, sliced
1 peach or nectarine, pitted and sliced
1 small carrot, grated
1 Fuji apple, grated
2 cups chopped pea shoots or pea greens
2 cups baby spinach
1 cup mint leaves
1 cup walnut pieces

1. Cover sliced red onion with cold water and set aside. (This removes some of the oil and mellows the onion's harshness.)

2. In a small bowl, combine feta, mayonnaise, honey, salt, pepper, and za'atar. Mix well and adjust seasoning as needed. Set aside.

3. In a large bowl, combine peas, cucumber, peach, carrot, apple, and drained onion. Toss to combine.

4. Spread pea shoots, spinach, and mint onto serving platter and top with the fruit and vegetables. Top with walnuts and dressing, or serve to your guests on the side.

Sinbad's Roc Egg Meatballs

Serves 8

The tales of Sinbad are told in several stories that recount his adventures, which all take a similar form. The ship runs aground, followed by terrible creatures and fates he and his crew must endure. They dock on an island that turns out to be a whale, land on a diamond-studded island teaming with giant birds (rocs), encounter snakes that can swallow elephants, are terrorized by one-eyed man-eating giants, meet bird-people, and discover streams and valleys laden with precious stones and pearls. In the end, Sinbad always returns to Basra very rich, only to quickly get bored and head out again.

In "The Fourth Voyage of Sinbad," the sailors come across a giant roc egg, which they crack open and eat. This results in an attack by the parent rocs, which are giant raptors that can carry away elephants. They pelt the ship with boulders, stranding the men on the island with no means of escape. There, the Old Man of the Sea enslaves Sinbad, but he eventually escapes and returns home with his fortune.

Real explorers also perpetuated the idea of giant birds. Marco Polo claimed to have seen one in Madagascar. Magellan's crew said they inhabited the China Sea region. And Chinese geographer Zhou Qufei pinpointed their location on a large island off of Africa. There are giant birds in the fossil record, but rather than looking like giant eagles, they were flightless and ostrich-like.

9 eggs, divided
6 cloves garlic
1 small yellow onion, grated
¼ cup chopped parsley
¼ cup chopped mint
1 tablespoon ground coriander
1 teaspoon ground cumin
1 teaspoon ground cardamom
½ teaspoon ground allspice
½ teaspoon cayenne pepper
¼ teaspoon ground ginger
1 pound ground beef
1 cup bulgur, soaked in hot water and drained
1 teaspoon sea salt
1 teaspoon black pepper
½ cup vegetable oil, or as needed
2 tablespoons za'atar
2 cups plain yogurt
¼ cup olive oil

1. Place 8 of the eggs in a pot of water to cover. Boil for 5 minutes, let sit in water off heat for 10 minutes, then shock in an ice bath. Peel and set aside.

2. Combine garlic, onion, herbs, and spices in a large bowl and mix well. Add beef, bulgur, salt, pepper, and remaining 1 egg, and stir or knead until ingredients are evenly distributed.

3. With wet hands, form egg-size balls of the seasoned ground beef. Flatten, then place a peeled hardboiled egg in the center. Press the ground meat around the egg and roll to completely conceal the egg. Repeat with remaining eggs and ground meat.

4. Heat cast-iron or other heavy skillet over high heat. Add about 1 tablespoon vegetable oil to lightly coat the bottom. Add several meatballs, but do not crowd them in. Cook, turning every couple of minutes, until browned on all sides. Remove from pan, and repeat with remaining meatballs.

5. Preheat oven to 350°F. Return all meatballs to the skillet. Mix together the za'atar, yogurt, and olive oil in a small bowl, and spread over the meatballs. Bake for 10 to 15 minutes, until the yogurt has browned. Serve warm.

Ali Baba's Open Sesame and Pistachio Halawa

Makes about 1 dozen pieces

This story, about a treasure in a cave accessible only by the secret magical words "open sesame" is, more than anything, a tale of greed and loyalty. There are great riches, terrifying outlaws, and dubious in-laws. The best part is that the hero of the tale is not Ali Baba, but his slave girl, Morgiana, who is smarter than everyone. Thankfully, she is rewarded in the end with freedom.

Halawa, or halva, is a dense, sweet cake made from ground nuts and seeds. Packed with protein, it's a great, guilt-free dessert. There are many versions in the Middle East, North Africa, the Balkans, and China. Sometimes it's made with flour, as in a semolina-based Indian version; it's also made with legumes and squash. But in the United States it is a tahini-nut version that is most prevalent. Tahini, a sesame seed butter, is readily available in most large supermarkets and from Middle Eastern grocers.

¾ cup shelled pistachios
½ cup granulated sugar
½ cup honey
¼ cup water
8 ounces raw tahini
Pinch sea salt
1 teaspoon vanilla extract

1. Coat a 6- to 8-inch springform pan with nonstick spray, and line with enough parchment or plastic wrap to fold over the edge (this pan will not go into the oven). Preheat oven to 350°F. Spread pistachios out in a single layer on a dry baking sheet, and roast until golden and fragrant, about 10 minutes. Cool completely. When cool, chop them finely by hand or in a food processor. Set aside.

2. Combine sugar, honey, and water in a large saucepan. Bring to a boil. Clip a candy thermometer to the side of the pot and cook to soft-ball stage (240°F).

3. Meanwhile, combine tahini, salt, and vanilla in a bowl. Beat together with a whisk. Slowly add the hot syrup while beating, whipping until fully incorporated. Fold in all but ½ cup of pistachios. Transfer to prepared plastic wrap-lined springform pan, top with remaining pistachios, and refrigerate. Chill for 24 hours before cutting into wedges. This resting time is necessary for the halawa to develop the hallmark crystalline structure that creates this confection's texture.

3
Shakespeare's Sorcery

Shakespeare's work is riddled with sorcery and witchcraft. Entertaining to us now, these inclusions resonated differently in sixteenth-century England, when witchcraft was considered the root of tragedy and illness—the devil's work. Even if someone recovered from sickness, recovery itself was considered proof that the original illness was caused by magic. The crime of magic carried punishments from pillory to execution.

Malleus Maleficarum, or *Hammer of Witches*, printed in 1487, was a guidebook for hunting and punishing witches. Most witchcraft inquiries were directed at women, considered more susceptible because they were weak, petty, and prone to gossip. Elderly women were persecuted in the greatest number (not young, pretty girls), probably because they were quicker to temper, with a tendency to lash out. Mischief caused by angry old ladies was obvious witchery. Witchcraft confessions were extracted through torture, often worse than the punishment itself, and women were encouraged to turn in others for leniency. Witch burning was fairly uncommon, however. Rather, they would be stoned to death or hanged. Witchcraft and magical acts performed in Shakespeare's work would have intensified fear of harm by witches, even in the theatergoing upper classes. Queen Elizabeth I believed that image magic, similar to use of a voodoo doll, was being used against her. Her courtier, Sir Walter Raleigh, concurred.

Pretty Little Chickens with Spring Onions

Serves 4

This play is the tale of a Scottish general influenced by a trio of witches that prophesized he would become king. Obsessed with ambition, Macbeth believed them, and they tricked him into believing he was invincible. Lady Macbeth was on board with the prophecy, and in an attempt to make herself like the witches, she called on the powers of darkness to unsex her—to make her old and menopausal, as it was elderly women who were the known witches. Macbeth, influenced by the witches and his wife, indeed murders the king and takes the crown. But in the end, we learn that being drunk with power doesn't pay.

It's thought the play itself was cursed by witches objecting to Shakespeare's research into real magic (some believe the chants and curses he used were from real witches). One must never utter the title of the play within a theater, lest he suffer injury, or worse. The first sign of this occurred during its first performance, when the actor playing Lady Macbeth died, forcing Shakespeare to perform the role. Other mishaps included actors falling off the stage, near misses from falling equipment, and a real dagger replacing the stage prop in a scene, causing the death of the actor. Then there's the Astor Place riot in 1849, pitting companies and fans of two New York productions against each other, causing twenty deaths. The antidote to utterance of the title is to exit the theater, spin three times, spit, curse, and knock on the theater door to be let back in.

The witches warn that Macduff, a nobleman hostile to Macbeth's claim to the throne, is dangerous, and so Macbeth has Macduff's family murdered. Macduff laments the loss of his children, described in the original text as "pretty little chickens." Basing a dish on this scene may seem gruesome, but then again, *Macbeth* is a gruesome play.

1 cup bitter orange marmalade

¼ cup brandy

1 cup orange juice, divided

2 oranges, zested and quartered

4 game hens, rinsed and patted dry

1 teaspoon sea salt

½ teaspoon cracked black pepper

1 teaspoon herbes de Provence

1 bunch fresh sage

1 bunch fresh thyme

1 bunch fresh Italian parsley

4 shallots, peeled and halved

1. Preheat oven to 375°F. In a small saucepan, combine marmalade, brandy, ½ cup of the orange juice, and orange zest. Bring to a boil, then reduce heat to a simmer. Cook until the liquid is reduced and the mixture has a thick glaze consistency, about 15 minutes. Set aside to cool.

2. Season hens inside and out with salt, pepper, and herbes de Provence. Trim stems off fresh herbs and use the stems to line the bottom of a roasting pan. Place shallots on top of herb stems. Add remaining orange juice to the pan. Divide herb leaves equally into four bundles. Insert one into each hen cavity, along with 2 orange quarters. Place hens on top of herb stems. Place in oven.

3. Roast hens for 1 hour, or until internal temperature reaches 165°F on a meat thermometer, brushing with marmalade glaze every 15 minutes. If skin darkens too quickly, tent with foil. Rest for 10 minutes, remove foil, and serve.

Rhubarb Pickles in Port

Makes about 1 quart

Though a force of Englishmen advanced on his castle at Dunsinane Hill, Macbeth was confident. The witches assured him he needn't fear death unless by the hand of someone not born of a woman, or "until Birnam Wood marches to fight you at Dunsinane Hill." Since all men are born of women, and a forest can't be moved, Macbeth felt safe. However, after the murder of Lady Macduff and the general Banquo (whose children were prophesied to inherit the throne), Lady Macbeth descended into madness, sleepwalking and complaining of bloodstains. Macbeth ordered the doctor to cure her of this illness—and sarcastically inquired about a cure for the advancing English. "What rhubarb, senna, or what purgative drug, would scour these English hence?" Seems he was not so confident after all.

1 pound rhubarb trimmed to
2-3 inches in length
3 shallots, sliced
3-4 bay leaves
5-6 pieces of thinly sliced ginger
¼ cup port or rum
1 cup water
1 cup cider vinegar
¾ cup sugar
4 cloves
Pinch crushed red pepper flakes
1 teaspoon sea salt
1 cinnamon stick, crushed
2 star anise, crushed
1 teaspoon toasted coriander seed
Grated zest of 1 orange

1. Pack trimmed rhubarb vertically in a quart container with a tight-fitting lid. Intersperse them with sliced shallots, bay leaves, and ginger. Set aside.

2. In a saucepan, combine remaining ingredients and bring to a boil. Cool slightly, then pour into the rhubarb container. Make sure the rhubarb is submerged. Cool to room temperature, then seal. Refrigerate 2 to 3 days. Serve with charcuterie, chop them into relish, mix into chicken salad, or use them to accompany rich meat and seafood. Pickles will keep for several weeks.

Macbeth

Witches' Brew (Coconut Shrimp Green Curry)

Serves 6-8

One suspected reason for the *Macbeth* curse was that the brew ingredients—fenny snake, eye of newt, and toe of frog—were thought to have come from real spells. The brew was made all the more real because the use of cauldrons was common. Few people had ovens (there was typically one large oven shared by the village to bake bread), and most cooking was done in cauldrons over an open fire. What set this recipe in the realm of witchcraft were the ingredients. The witches included strange and foreign items, including animals not usually consumed (dog, bat, owl), weird animal parts (eye of newt, toe of frog, baboon blood), and parts of foreigners (Jew's liver, Tartar's lips, Turk's nose). This recipe contains none of those elements, but it does have an eerie, demonic look about it. But don't be put off. This curry is delicious.

2 tablespoons coconut oil
1 teaspoon sesame oil
1 red onion, minced
5 green onions, chopped
3 cloves garlic
One 1-inch piece ginger, grated
1 stalk lemongrass, cut into 1-inch segments
1 cup diced purple carrot
5 purple yams, peeled and diced
¼ cup green curry paste
1 teaspoon ground cumin
1 teaspoon sea salt
One 14-ounce can coconut milk
4 cups vegetable, chicken, or fish broth
1 pound medium raw shrimp, peeled and deveined
2 cups cooked black rice (also known as forbidden rice)
Grated zest and juice of 1 lime, plus 1 lime cut into wedges
½ cup cilantro leaves, chopped
1 tablespoon toasted sesame seeds

1. Melt coconut and sesame oils in a large cauldron (or heavy-bottomed soup pot). Add red and green onions, garlic, ginger, lemongrass, carrot, and yams, and sauté until they begin to brown. Add curry paste, cumin, and salt, and toast briefly.

2. Add coconut milk and broth. Bring to a boil. At the boil, reduce heat. Simmer 10 minutes until potatoes are tender. Add shrimp, rice, and lime zest and juice. Cook 5 minutes, until shrimp are cooked through. Fish out the lemongrass and serve with fresh cilantro, sesame seeds, and lime wedges.

Ferdinand's Punishment (Mussels in Corn Broth)

Serves 4

Often considered Shakespeare's most magical play, *The Tempest* explores themes of violence and love. Overthrown from his seat as Duke of Milan by his brother Antonio, Prospero is exiled to an island with his daughter, Miranda. He uses magic and the help of the spirit Ariel, to conjure a great storm (a tempest), causing the wreck of a ship that carries Antonio and the king of Naples, Alonso.

This story is full of magic, but the real story is the power of knowledge. Prospero's magic is not naturally occurring, but rather scientifically attained through secret studies. This idea was popular in the early seventeenth century, when the play was written. Science was considered radical, well beyond the understanding of most people. The conflation of science and magic is represented here, and Prospero's exile reflects the poor treatment of science, especially by the church.

Magic represents control for Prospero, whether it is dark magic or a love charm. Prospero's plan was to have Ferdinand, the son of Alonso, king of Naples, fall in love with Miranda. They did indeed fall in love at first sight, which pleased Prospero. But to prevent them from moving too quickly, he accused Ferdinand of being an imposter. As Ferdinand drew his sword, Prospero cast a spell and took Ferdinand prisoner. He was fed a diet of brook mussels, withered roots, and acorn husks. Mussels were considered poor man's food well into the twentieth century, though modern palates have found much pleasure in these mollusks.

2 tablespoons unsalted butter
4 red new potatoes, quartered
4 green onions, chopped
1 fennel bulb, sliced
2 cups fresh or frozen corn kernels
1 pint cherry tomatoes, halved
5 cloves garlic, minced, divided
1 teaspoon sea salt
½ teaspoon cracked black pepper
2 red bell peppers, diced
3 pounds mussels, scrubbed and beards removed
2 cups dry white wine
Pinch saffron threads
Grated zest of 1 lemon
½ cup Italian parsley, chopped
8 slices crusty French bread

1. Heat butter in a large, heavy soup pot over high heat. Add potatoes, green onions, fennel, corn, and tomatoes. Cook, stirring, until browned. Reduce heat to low and add 3 cloves of the garlic. Cook for another 2 minutes. Add salt, pepper, and red peppers. Stir to combine and simmer for 10 minutes, covered.

2. Add mussels, white wine, and saffron. Turn the heat down to a low simmer and cover tightly. Steam for 10 to 15 minutes, until the shells are opened.

3. Meanwhile, mince together lemon zest, parsley, and remaining 2 cloves garlic. To serve, divide mussels among four bowls, top with parsley mixture, and serve with sliced French bread.

Caliban's Hot Crab Dip with Tropical Fruit Salsa

Serves 8-10

Caliban is described as a deformed monster, sometimes half fish, half tortoise, or dwarf. He is the son of the Sycorax, an Algerian witch who was banished to the island and died before Prospero's arrival. Prospero entrapped and enslaved Caliban, then mocked and mistreated him. The characters of Caliban and Prospero run parallel—Prospero took the island from Caliban, Antonio took Milan from Prospero—and hint at the cruelty of colonialism, rampant in Europe at the time.

Caliban meets jester Trinculo and butler Stephano, who mock him but are friendly, finding common ground on the low rung of the social ladder. They give him drink and do not torment him too badly, so Caliban is eager to leave Prospero and become their servant. He offers to show them where all the best food on the island can be found: "Let me bring thee where crabs grow. And I with my long nails will dig thee pignuts, show thee a jay's nest, . . . bring thee to clustering filberts." This recipe is inspired by the offer, and the island.

1 cup cream cheese
½ cup mayonnaise
½ cup sour cream
4 green onions, chopped
1 clove garlic, minced
1 teaspoon dried thyme
½ teaspoon cayenne pepper
½ teaspoon cracked black pepper
1 tablespoon Worcestershire sauce
1 tablespoon Dijon mustard
Two 6-ounce cans lump crabmeat
4 ounces grated Cheddar cheese
1 cup chopped pineapple
1 cup chopped mango
1 cup chopped cucumber
¼ cup chopped red onion
Grated zest and juice of 1 lime
¼ cup chopped cilantro
Pinch sea salt

1. Preheat oven to 350°F. In a large bowl, beat cream cheese, mayonnaise, and sour cream together until smooth, and lump free. Add green onions, garlic, thyme, cayenne, black pepper, Worcestershire, mustard, crab, and cheese. Mix thoroughly. Transfer to a cast-iron skillet and bake for 20 to 30 minutes, until browned and bubbly.

2. Meanwhile, in a bowl, toss together pineapple, mango, cucumber, red onion, lime zest and juice, and cilantro. Season with salt and set aside.

3. To serve, top the hot crab skillet with the cool fruit salsa. Serve with tortilla chips or baguette slices.

Ariel's Ginger-Lime Bars

Makes about 1 dozen

Ariel is a spirit Prospero found trapped by a witch in a tree on the island. In return for rescue, Ariel promises to serve Prospero for a year. She acted as his eyes and ears and performed magical feats, including creating the titular storm as well as the love between Miranda and Ferdinand. Such spirits were described in a number of ways during the Renaissance—as agents of the devil, or of God, or in a more scientific way, able to be controlled by wise men. Shakespeare's version of such a spirit is unusual in that it has human characteristics, acting on behalf of Prospero to right wrongs that were perpetrated against him. But it is clear that Ariel is helping only so that he will be set free from Prospero's service.

Staging of Ariel's magic scenes was elaborate for the time. They included wires, trapdoors, and dramatic costume changes. The most dramatic of these scenes is Prospero's banquet (act 3, scene 3). Alonso and his courtiers search for his son, Ferdinand, (whom they thought lost at sea—the audience knows he is alive and well, in love with Miranda). Exhausted, they are suddenly presented with a magical feast, brought to them by a procession of magical creatures. On the direction of Prospero, Ariel suddenly appears in a clap of thunder, dressed as a harpy (a bird of prey with a woman's face). He makes the banquet magically disappear and confronts the men with their crime—driving Prospero from Milan. For this sin, says Ariel, the power of nature has taken revenge on Ferdinand. There is no mention of the food presented by the spirits, but because the island is exotic, it's likely these bars were among the offerings.

CRUST

1 cup (2 sticks, 8 ounces) unsalted butter
½ cup granulated sugar
2 cups all-purpose flour
½ teaspoon sea salt

TOPPING

1½ cups granulated sugar
4 large eggs
Grated zest of 2 limes
¾ cup lime juice
2 tablespoons freshly grated ginger
¼ cup all-purpose flour
Powdered sugar for dusting

1. To make the crust: Preheat oven to 375°F. Coat a 9 x 13-inch baking pan with nonstick spray. In a stand mixer, or in a bowl using a handheld mixer, cream together butter and granulated sugar until smooth and lump free. Add flour and salt and mix just until a dough is formed. Press into the prepared pan and bake for 10 to 15 minutes, until golden brown.

2. To make the topping: In a bowl, mix together granulated sugar, eggs, lime zest, lime juice, and ginger. Stir in flour and whisk until smooth. Reduce the oven temperature to 350°F and pour the lime mixture on top of the baked crust. Return to oven for 30 minutes, until just browned and set. Cool, and then refrigerate until firm. To serve, slice into squares and dust with powdered sugar.

Apple of Demetrius's Eye Love Potion

Serves 2

Possibly Shakespeare's most popular play, *A Midsummer Night's Dream* is full of magic, mischief, and love. It takes place in a forest on the eve of the marriage of Theseus, Duke of Athens, to Hippolyta, Queen of the Amazons. In the woods, four lovers are caught in a messy set of affairs. Hermia and Lysander are in love and plan to be married, though their match is against her father's wish for her to marry Demetrius. Demetrius, who once loved Hermia's friend Helena, becomes jealous of Lysander for wooing Hermia, and wants her for himself. Helena becomes jealous of Demetrius's attention.

Meanwhile, the Fairy King, Oberon, and his queen, Titania, argue over a changeling boy who takes all of her affection. In fairy lore, a changeling is a human child stolen and replaced with a fairy child. Titania loves the child, but Oberon wants the boy as his servant, so he devises a plan to use a love potion to steal the changeling boy from Titania. The magic will make her love another obsessively, distracting her so that Oberon can steal the boy. His plan requires help from a fairy, Robin Goodfellow (nicknamed Puck). Puck puts the love potion on Titania, and then, since he has the potion anyway, tries to make Demetrius fall in love with Helena–except something goes wrong.

At the start of the play, Helena chases after Demetrius, who is pursuing Hermia. She tells him of Hermia and Lysander's plan to marry. Puck, hoping to stop the commotion, plans to use the love potion, made for Titania, to bring Helena and Demetrius together again. But Puck puts the potion on Lysander by mistake. Realizing this, he puts it on Demetrius, too. When they wake up, they both fall in love with Helena, the first person they see. However, the love from the potion is not a sweet love, but an obsessive one. In their confusion, the men want to fight for Helena, and Hermia wants to fight Helena for stealing Lysander. The root of all the trouble between the humans is Demetrius, and his constant pursuit of Hermia, which throws love out of balance, and disrupts the wood. If you have a Demetrius in your life, try this recipe. If nothing else, it will cheer you up for a bit!

Small amount of cider vinegar
Cinnamon sugar
6 ounces apple cider
2 ounces rum
2 ounces Calvados brandy
6 ounces ginger beer or ginger ale
1 apple, sliced into thin half moons

1. Coat the rim of two 6- to 8-ounce cocktail glasses with cider vinegar, then dip in cinnamon sugar to coat the rims.

2. Combine apple cider, rum, and Calvados with 4 to 5 ice cubes in a cocktail shaker. Shake to blend. Strain into prepared glasses. Top off with ginger beer and garnish with an apple wheel.

Bottom's Giant Ox Beef Short Ribs

Serves 4

In *A Midsummer Night's Dream*, a troupe of actors rehearses a play they plan to perform during the wedding festivities for Theseus and Hippolyta. Bottom, a weaver, has a part, but also ideas and opinions. He has self-confidence, to be sure, but is not the brightest bulb, often using language incorrectly and making silly mistakes. Puck, who enjoys pulling pranks on humans, thinks Bottom a ridiculous, terrible actor, so he changes Bottom's head into that of an ass. Bottom's friends run in terror, but he thinks it is a trick, so he begins singing to show that he is not afraid. This music wakes up Titania, whose eyes are dosed with Oberon's love potion. As is the case with Demetrius and Lysander, the effect is a passionate, obsessive love for the first thing seen upon waking. The first thing she sees is Bottom, and she falls desperately in love with him, ass's head and all.

Bottom is unaware that he has the head of an ass. And although he is a humble weaver, he is not phased one bit by the fact that the Queen of the Fairies has suddenly, for no apparent reason, declared love for him. This scene demonstrates the height of arrogance and foolishness, for during the Renaissance, love between classes was more scandalous than relations with a donkey.

Titania calls on her fairies—Peaseblossom, Cobweb, Moth, and Mustardseed—to take care of Bottom. As they introduce themselves, he makes conversation, sending his regards to Peaseblossom's parents, and to Mustardseed, he laments the loss of all the little mustard seeds used as a condiment for "giant-like Ox-Beef."

½ cup dried shiitake mushrooms
2 cups warm water
½ cup olive oil, divided
4 beef short ribs
1 cup all-purpose flour
1 yellow onion, diced
1 large carrot, diced
2 stalks celery, diced
3 cups chopped cremini or wild mushrooms (when available)
¼ cup seeded mustard
2 cloves garlic, minced
2 sprigs fresh thyme
1 bay leaf
1 teaspoon chopped fresh sage
1 teaspoon sea salt
3 cups dry white wine
2 cups fresh or frozen peas
½ cup chopped Italian parsley
Sliced French bread for serving

1. In a bowl, cover dried shiitake mushrooms with warm water and set aside to reconstitute. (This step may be done several hours ahead.)

2. Heat half the oil in a large, heavy soup pot over high heat. Dredge beef short ribs in flour, shake off excess, and brown in oil on all sides. Do this in batches, careful not to crowd the pan. When browned, remove from pot, and set aside.

3. Preheat oven to 300°F. In the same pan, heat remaining oil. Add onion, carrot, and celery, and sauté, stirring, until translucent, about 10 minutes. Add chopped fresh mushrooms and continue to sauté, stirring. Strain the reconstituted dried mushrooms (reserving their liquid), chop, and add to the pot along with mustard, garlic, thyme, bay leaf, sage, and salt. Stir well.

4. Add short ribs back to the pot. Add wine and reserved mushroom water. Bring to a boil, remove from heat, cover tightly with a lid, and bake for 2 hours. Check the shanks for tenderness. They should be easily falling off the bone. If not, return to the oven for another 30 to 60 minutes. Add the peas during the last 10 minutes of cooking. Remove the bay leaf and thyme sprigs and discard.

Serve warm, with a sprinkle of chopped parsley and crusty French bread to spread the marrow on. This also goes nicely over mashed potatoes.

Titania's Apricot and Dewberry Crisp

Serves 4-6

According to English lore, the Queen of the Fairies has the true power, not the King. The quarrel between Titania and her husband, Oberon—the one who catalyzes the events of our story—would have been viewed by a sixteenth-century audience differently than we do today. They would have anticipated an outcome in which everyone figured out what happened and in which Oberon got in big trouble. In her infatuation with Bottom, Titania instructs her fairies to, "feed him with apricots and dewberries, with purple grapes, green figs, and mulberries." Sure, Bottom is an arrogant fool and has an ass's head, but at least he is not Oberon.

Dewberries are related to blackberries but are shaped like raspberries. For this recipe, you may substitute either berry—or a combination of both—if dewberries are not available.

12 large apricots, pitted and cut into thin wedges
2 pints dewberries, blackberries, or raspberries
3 tablespoons honey
½ teaspoon ground cardamom
½ teaspoon freshly grated nutmeg
Grated zest of 1 lemon
2 pinches sea salt, divided
1 cup plus 2 tablespoons all-purpose flour, divided
½ cup rolled oats
¼ cup granulated sugar
½ cup brown sugar
½ cup (1 stick, 4 ounces) unsalted butter
Vanilla ice cream for serving

1. Preheat oven to 350°F. Coat a 9 x13-inch pan with nonstick spray. In a large bowl, combine apricots, dewberries, and honey and toss to coat thoroughly. Add cardamom, nutmeg, lemon zest, and 1 pinch salt and toss to coat. Add 2 tablespoons of the flour, toss to coat, and transfer to prepared pan.

2. In the same bowl, mix together remaining 1 cup flour, oats, sugars, and remaining pinch salt. Cut in the butter until the mixture resembles thick crumbs. Spread out crumb topping evenly over the top of the fruit. Bake for 30 to 45 minutes until fruit is bubbly and crumbs are golden brown. Serve spoonfuls of crisp in bowls, topped with a generous scoop of vanilla ice cream.

In the end, Oberon tells Puck to reverse the potion's effects on Titania and Lysander and to fix Bottom's head. When he does so, everyone thinks the events of the night were a dream. Everyone is paired, and happy. Both couples go back to Athens to wed, along with Theseus and Hippolyta.

4

Tolkien Universe

In 1937, John Ronald Reuel (J.R.R.) Tolkien published what was meant to be a children's fantasy adventure novel, called *The Hobbit: or There and Back Again*. The book was initially written for his children, but through a friend of a friend, it came to the attention of the London publishing world and became as popular with adults as with children, thus warranting a sequel, *The Lord of the Rings*. The three-volume sequel took more than ten years to complete and has become one of the most popular trilogies ever written. Intended again for children, the sequel had a darker, more serious tone.

What followed, along with other writings that included children's stories and classic translations, was a number of backstories written throughout his life, referred to as the *Legendarium* and published posthumously by his son. Tolkien drew upon mythology as well as medieval epics in creating his narratives. The Tolkien universe is comprised of a number of stories presented in a variety of forms that were directly influenced by, and make reference to, these works. It is safe to say that every story, film, game, song, and painting that is set in a medieval fantasy world of swords and sorcery is directly or indirectly inspired by the work of Tolkien. Here, we will look at a few of the most famous sword-and-sorcery narratives that are derived, or influenced by, Tolkien.

Gandalf's Cold Chicken and Pickles

Serves 6-8

The first successful Tolkien epic, *The Hobbit: or There and Back Again*, initiated the world known as Arda and the land of Middle-earth, inhabited by men, hobbits, elves, dwarves, wizards, divinities, demons, ghouls, and monsters. The story follows the quest of a hobbit (a short humanoid with furry feet) named Bilbo Baggins to reclaim a treasure guarded by the dragon Smaug, culminating in an epic Battle of the Five Armies (partly based on Tolkien's own experience in World War I).

When the Wizard Gandalf arrives at Bilbo's door, Bilbo is suspicious, declining an invitation to an adventure. But, not to seem rude, Bilbo invites Gandalf to tea sometime. The next day, Bilbo's doorbell rings, presumably Gandalf again, but it's a dwarf, who invites himself in and asks for food. Soon, more dwarves arrive, as does Gandalf. They eat up Bilbo's pantry before describing the adventure they are about to undertake. Though he protests (hobbits are homebodies, not prone to adventure), Bilbo joins them on their quest to reclaim the dwarves' kingdom and treasure, usurped by the dragon Smaug.

The scene of this unexpected party describes Bilbo's abundant larder, when thirteen dwarves and one wizard demand ale, porter, coffee, cakes, scones, raspberry jam, apple tart, mince pie, cheese, pork pie, and salad. And seeming to already know it is available, Gandalf asks to, "bring out the cold chicken and pickles!" Such a dish was considered a treat in the Victorian era, as roasting an animal was reserved for celebrations. Cold leftovers were coveted, especially in sandwich form. The meal fit into the setting of the Shire, modeled on, as Tolkien himself stated, "more or less a Warwickshire village of about the period of (Queen Victoria's) Diamond Jubilee" of the late nineteenth century.

Interestingly, in Tolkien's first edition, Gandalf asked for chicken and tomatoes. The change to pickles was among many rewritten sections of the second edition, more in keeping with the universe backstory (*Legendarium*) that Tolkien was constantly creating. This recipe is a modern riff on the chicken and pickle theme, using the brine of the pickle to enhance the moist, savory flavors and give the dish that Middle-earth zing.

6-8 pieces bone-in chicken
(breast, legs, or thighs)
2 cups dill pickle brine
2 teaspoons sea salt, divided
Freshly cracked black pepper
1 tablespoon dried dill, divided
2 teaspoons celery seed, divided
2 tablespoons red wine vinegar
1 tablespoon honey
2 dill pickles, sliced into thin wheels
½ red onion, sliced
4 large radishes, sliced into thin wheels
1 English or 2 Persian cucumbers,
sliced into thin wheels
¼ cup chopped fresh dill

1. Combine chicken and dill pickle brine in a large zip-top bag or bowl. Refrigerate for 12 to 24 hours (longer is better).

2. Preheat oven to 475°F. Place chicken in baking dish. Sprinkle with a pinch of salt and pepper and 1 teaspoon each dried dill and celery seed. Bake for 20-30 minutes, until skin is brown and crispy (internal temperature should reach 165°F on a meat thermometer). Cool to room temperature. Chill completely in refrigerator (this can be done a day ahead).

3. Meanwhile, make the quick pickles. In a large bowl, mix remaining salt, dried dill, celery seed, vinegar, and honey. Add pickles, onion, radishes, and cucumbers. Toss to coat. Refrigerate for 1 to 2 hours. To serve, garnish chicken with chopped fresh dill, and quick-pickled vegetables.

Shire Seed Cakes

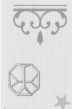

Makes 8

Thinking the knock at the door is Gandalf, Bilbo sets out another cup and a cake or two for tea. But he opens it to find a dwarf, who invites himself in, asking for beer and "seed-cake if you have any. Lots!" Having prepared himself for a sophisticated affair, Bilbo is dismayed to find it turning into a style of tea enjoyed by common working folk. The scene likely rang more comedic to the English of the late 1930s, who would have been well aware of the stark differences between high and low tea.

A recipe for such cake can be found in the Victorian cookbook and home manual *Mrs. Beeton's Book of Household Management*, published in 1861. It seems likely a recipe Tolkien enjoyed himself as a child. The ingredients are inexpensive and easily obtainable year-round. The cakes themselves are filling and last for several days. In fact, Bilbo baked two "beautiful round seed-cakes" that afternoon. This recipe is closer to modern tastes, with a heartier, more generous helping of healthful seeds and a more scone-like texture than Mrs. Beeton intended.

2 cups all-purpose flour
½ cup whole wheat four
½ cup rolled oats
¼ cup toasted pumpkin seeds (pepitas)
2 tablespoons sesame seeds
2 tablespoons sunflower seeds
1 tablespoon poppy seeds
⅓ cup brown sugar
1 tablespoon baking powder
1 teaspoon ground nutmeg
½ teaspoon ground cinnamon
1 teaspoon sea salt
1 cup (2 sticks, 8 ounces) unsalted butter, diced
1 egg
½ cup milk
¼ cup heavy cream
2 tablespoons granulated sugar

1. Preheat oven to 350°F. Line a baking sheet with parchment paper.

2. In a large bowl, combine flours, oats, seeds, brown sugar, baking powder, nutmeg, cinnamon, and salt. Mix to combine thoroughly. Cut in butter to pea-size pieces, until the mixture resembles a coarse meal.

3. In a small, separate bowl, combine egg and milk. Make a well in the center of the flour mixture, and pour in the milk. Using a fork, mix until the dough just comes together.

4. Turn the dough out onto a floured work surface and knead three or four times to bring all the dry bits together, then pat down into a disk 1-inch thick. Using a knife, cut the disk into 8 wedges. Transfer to the prepared baking sheet. Brush each wedge with cream. Sprinkle the tops with granulated sugar. Rest cakes for 10 minutes before baking for 15 to 20 minutes, until golden brown. Serve with butter and jam.

The Prancing Pony's Blackberry Tart

Serves 6-8

The Lord of the Rings, a sequel to *The Hobbit*, was published in three volumes, from 1954 to 1955. *The Fellowship of the Ring*, *The Two Towers*, and *The Return of the King* follow Frodo Baggins, who inherits a ring from his cousin Bilbo. Gandalf the Wizard determines it's the One Ring possessing the power to conquer Middle-earth, thus starting the quest by Frodo and friends to save civilization from evil. Gandalf convinces Frodo to take the ring to the Elven valley of Rivendell, and the Council of the Wise, where it's decided it must be destroyed at Mount Doom, in the evil realm of Mordor. A fellowship is formed, including four hobbits, Gandalf, the man Aragorn, Legolas the Elf, Gimli the Dwarf, and the man Boromir, son of the ruler of the land of Gondor. The Elf queen, Galadriel, gives them gifts to aid their quest, but Gollum, an ancient creature who wants the ring, tracks their progress. The quest takes our heroes across Middle-earth, where they experience strange creatures and epic battles. It's a classic example of the hero's journey—adventure, crisis, victory, and transformation.

In Middle-earth, the Prancing Pony Inn is a common layover for men, dwarves, and hobbits. It's also here that we find some delightful culinary descriptions. "In a twinkling the table was laid. There was hot soup, cold meats, a blackberry tart, new loaves, slabs of butter, and half a ripe cheese: good plain food."

PÂTE SUCRÉE

1 cup (2 sticks, 8 oz.) unsalted butter
½ cup granulated sugar
1 large egg
3 cups cake or all-purpose flour
Uncooked rice or dried beans
(for weighing down the crust
while baking)

FILLING AND TOPPING

6 pints blackberries, divided
3 eggs
¾ cup granulated sugar
½ teaspoon sea salt
1½ cups cream
1 teaspoon vanilla extract
Powdered sugar for dusting

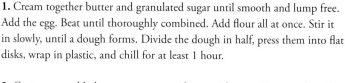

1. Cream together butter and granulated sugar until smooth and lump free. Add the egg. Beat until thoroughly combined. Add flour all at once. Stir it in slowly, until a dough forms. Divide the dough in half, press them into flat disks, wrap in plastic, and chill for at least 1 hour.

2. Coat a removable-bottom tart pan with nonstick spray. Dust work surface with flour. Pinch off enough dough for one tart shell (about one-third). Knead briefly to soften, pat into a disk (start round, end round), and roll out into a circle a couple inches larger than the pan no more than ¼-inch thick.

3. Preheat oven to 350°F. Line the tart pan, pressing the dough into place, pinching off the top rim flush with the rim of the pan. If the dough cracks or tears, simply patch it as needed. When your shell is lined, freeze it for at least 10 minutes. Line the frozen shell with parchment paper. Fill with uncooked rice or dried beans to weigh it down. Blind bake for 10 to 15 minutes, until just golden. Cool, and then remove the parchment and rice.

4. To make the filling, puree 4 pints of the blackberries in a blender, then strain into a large bowl. Add eggs, granulated sugar, and salt. Whisk until smooth. Add cream and vanilla. Stir to combine. Pour custard into prebaked shell. Bake at 325°F for about 30 minutes, or until custard is just set and has a jiggle to it. Cool completely. Refrigerate for at least 1 hour.

5. To serve, cover the top of the tart with remaining 2 pints fresh blackberries and dust with powdered sugar.

Dungeons & Dragons

Acorn Soup

Serves 4-6

Dungeons & Dragons is a tabletop role-playing game that grew out of traditional war games played by noblemen to master warfare. Like chess, the first incarnations from the eighteenth century used model figures of military units, competing on a grid representing geographical terrain. With the resurgence of Tolkien's popularity in the 1960s, two game developers, Gary Gygax and Dave Arneson, created this medieval role-playing game that included hobbits (later changed to halflings), elves, dwarves, and orcs. Its innovation was in giving players the ability to create their own characters.

The heart of Dungeons & Dragons is storytelling. There are structured stories, but players create their characters. Rolling the dice determines which routes players take, consequences of actions, and storylines. With friends, they explore, solve puzzles, battle monsters, discover magic, and hunt for treasure. The game exists in a cosmos of innumerable worlds called the Multiverse. Some settings are well known in the game, while individual players create others. A game's leader, the Dungeon Master, referees the game. The DM can also improvise in response to what adventurers do, making the game unexpected and exciting. As monsters are defeated and treasures recovered, players amass power. A quest can take place in one sitting or last for years.

Eating is part of the game, because one needs strength on a quest. Some food might simply be described as rations or divided by status (poor, modest, or comfortable rations). The official *Player's Handbook* also describes possible foodstuffs. Inspired by Tolkien, the fare is decidedly English. The following is an inexpensive soup, necessary for sustenance, though fit for a king.

2 acorn squash, halved and seeded
2-4 tablespoons olive oil, plus extra for garnish
1 bulb garlic, unpeeled
1 cup sliced almonds
1 yellow onion, diced
1 stalk celery, diced
½ teaspoon ground cinnamon
1 teaspoon ground cumin
1 teaspoon sea salt
½ teaspoon cracked black pepper
2 cups vegetable or chicken broth
1 cup half-and-half
1 cup sour cream
1 tablespoon toasted sesame seeds
1 tablespoon pumpkin seeds (pepitas)

1. Preheat oven to 375°F. Place squash in a baking dish, cut-side up, and brush with olive oil. Bake for 30 to 45 minutes, until browned and cooked through. Cool.

2. Meanwhile, wrap garlic bulb in foil and cook alongside the squash until tender, about 45 to 60 minutes. Cool.

3. In a heavy soup pot, heat remaining oil. Add almonds, onion, and celery. Sauté until golden brown. Add cinnamon, cumin, salt, and pepper. Scoop squash out of its skin and add to the pot. Squeeze garlic out of its skin and add it as well. Add broth and simmer on medium to warm through.

4. Puree the soup by using an immersion blender or by running it through a blender in batches (let the mixture cool a bit before using the blender). Return the puree to the stove, add half-and-half, and warm through. Serve with a dollop of sour cream, a drizzle of good olive oil, and seeds.

Wren Pot Pie with Cattails

Makes 6-8

This recipe has a high-status rating, because historically, anything served in a crust required the talents of a skilled baker. Though pie was a means of prolonging the shelf life of meat, here it has evolved into a more decadent presentation of the delicate wren. The wren, in real life, is not a game bird. It is a very small songbird that displays loud, complex songs. It is, however, pudgy looking, which suggests it could be delicious. The stem of a cattail, if peeled, is edible, and tastes a bit like a combination of cucumber and asparagus. But because you may not live near a marsh, this recipe defaults to asparagus. Feel free to substitute cattails if you are marsh adjacent.

4 tablespoons unsalted butter

1 yellow onion, diced

1 large carrot, diced

2 stalks celery, diced

2 cups cremini mushrooms, chopped

4 tablespoons all-purpose flour

2-3 cups chicken stock

1 teaspoon sea salt

½ teaspoon cracked black pepper

½ teaspoon chopped fresh sage

½ teaspoon dried thyme

½ teaspoon rosemary

Grated zest of 1 lemon

4 cups cooked and shredded squab, turkey, or chicken

8 ounces asparagus, cut into ½-inch pieces

1 cup grated Gruyère or Swiss cheese

1 package frozen puff pastry, defrosted overnight in the refrigerator

1 large egg, whisked

¼ cup grated Parmesan cheese

1. Melt butter in a large, heavy-bottomed soup pot over high heat. Add onion, carrot, and celery. Cook, stirring, until translucent, about 10 minutes. Add mushrooms and continue cooking until the mushrooms wilt and turn golden brown. Add flour and continue cooking, stirring, so that vegetables are well coated. Slowly add the stock, stirring. The addition of liquid to the roux will create the binding sauce (known as velouté).

2. Remove pot from heat. Add salt, pepper, sage, thyme, rosemary, and lemon zest. Stir thoroughly. Fold in squab and asparagus. Cool completely (this much can be done up to a day ahead).

3. Preheat oven to 350°F. Fill six to eight 12- to 14-ounce individual baking dishes to within ½ inch of the rim with the meat and vegetable filling. Top each with a generous pinch of Gruyère cheese. Cut puff pastry into squares large enough to cover the dishes (it's okay to have corners draping down the side a bit). Brush the top of the dough with egg and sprinkle with Parmesan. With a paring knife, slice through the pastry to create a few decorative steam vents. Place the dishes on a large baking sheet (to make getting them in and out of the oven easier). Bake for 30 to 40 minutes, rotating the baking sheet throughout baking to promote even browning, until the dough is golden brown and the filling is bubbly. Cool slightly before serving.

Dungeons & Dragons

Thistle Salad

Serves 8

The artichoke is the only thistle commonly used in cooking, though wild thistles are also edible. Like the cattail, the stems can be peeled, revealing the inner core that has a delicate, earthy flavor, similar to the artichoke. You need some thick gloves for this procedure, though, as thistle stems are just as pokey as the rest of the plant. So in lieu of this, the following is an artichoke recipe. You're welcome.

1 red onion, sliced
One 9-ounce package frozen artichoke hearts, defrosted, drained, patted dry, and quartered
2 cups walnut halves
2-3 cloves garlic, minced
1 teaspoon sea salt, or to taste
4 tablespoons olive oil, divided
½ cup Kalamata olives, sliced
2 tablespoons chopped fresh oregano
¼ cup chopped fresh mint
Grated zest and juice of 1 orange
Grated zest and juice of 1 lemon
1 Persian cucumber, diced
1 Fuji (or similar) apple, cored and diced
1 cup fresh or frozen (defrosted) peas
One 14-oz can hearts of palm, drained and sliced in wheels
4 cups arugula
4 ounces goat cheese

1. Preheat oven to 375°F. In a bowl, cover sliced onion with cold water (to remove harsh oils). Set aside. In a large bowl, combine artichoke hearts, walnuts, and garlic. Add salt and 1 tablespoon of the oil to lightly coat. Toss to thoroughly coat, and spread out on a baking sheet in a single layer. Roast for 10 to 20 minutes, until charred and fragrant. Cool.

2. In the same bowl, whisk together remaining 3 tablespoons oil with olives, oregano, mint, and citrus zest and juice. Season to taste with salt. Drain onion and add to the bowl along with cucumber, apple, peas, hearts of palm, and arugula. Toss to coat. Add cooled artichokes and walnuts. Toss again. Plate well-mixed portions of salad and top with crumbled goat cheese.

Forest Strider Drumstick

Serves 4

Tolkien-themed video games were popular in the 1980s through the 2000s. Among them, World of Warcraft is unique. First developed in 2004 by Blizzard Entertainment, WoW is a multiplayer role-playing game, similar in concept to Dungeons & Dragons. Players create and control their characters and inhabit complex worlds in which members of the Alliance (led by humans), or the Horde (led by orcs), interact with characters. A player's adventures take them from wild, untamed country populated by monsters and beasts to magnificent cities. Along the way, the players meet (and are called on to assist) heroes of legend. A player can choose to become a fierce warrior, master assassin, powerful wizard, and more. Players interact with millions of other players who also inhabit this virtual world, collaborating or competing along the way.

Food and drink have two purposes: to restore health lost in battle and to provide characters with additional abilities that increase their powers. Players acquire recipes in two ways: by purchasing them from in-game cooks, as rewards for completing quests or by trading with other players. Some recipes are very common and virtually universally known, with the ingredients being easy to obtain in the game. Other recipes are very rare and highly sought after, requiring ingredients only obtained with great effort. The following recipe, however, should not be too difficult to complete.

Forest Striders are big, two-legged, flightless birds that are not unlike ostriches in stance and gait. They have bright plumage and large beaks, reminiscent of birds from Earth's tropical rainforests. However, Forest Striders are only found in the haunted forest of Darkmoon Island, which has a temperate climate. This recipe has substituted turkey.

BRINE AND MEAT

1 quart water
1 onion, roughly chopped
1 cup sea salt
½ cup brown sugar
4 cloves garlic, minced
5 bay leaves
1 cinnamon stick
2 star anise pods
1 tablespoon mustard seeds
2 tablespoons black peppercorns, crushed
2 teaspoons juniper berries, crushed
1 teaspoon allspice berries, crushed
½ teaspoon cloves
4 turkey legs

RUB

2 tablespoons black pepper
2 tablespoons toasted and ground coriander
2 tablespoons toasted and ground mustard seeds
2 tablespoons paprika
2 tablespoons garlic powder
2 tablespoons onion powder
2 tablespoons brown sugar

1. In a large pot, combine water with the onion, salt, brown sugar, garlic, and spices. Bring the mixture to a boil, then simmer until the salt and sugar dissolve. Remove from heat. Pour into large container of at least a gallon capacity. Add a few cups of ice to accelerate cooling. Cool completely.

2. When cool, add turkey legs, taking care to submerge them, which may require a plate on top to weigh them down. Refrigerate for 24 to 48 hours. Flip the meat periodically to stir up the brine and ensure even absorption. It can stay in the brine for a much longer time, but it takes at least a day for the brine to penetrate.

3. Remove meat from brine (discard brine), place in another large container, and cover with cold water. Refrigerate 3 to 4 hours, or overnight, to remove the excess salt. Rinse and pat dry.

4. Preheat oven to 250° F. Place a rack inside a roasting pan.

5. Mix the rub spices. Massage them liberally into brined turkey legs. Place the meat on the rack. Fill with 1 inch of water. Cover tightly with a lid or foil. Roast for 4 to 5 hours, until the meat pulls away from the bone easily. Remove from oven and serve.

Baked Manta Ray

Serves 4

This dish, a specialty of the Vrykul of Northrend, is hearty and protein packed, and uses traditional flavors of that frozen land, including herbaceous spices. In our world, however, the manta ray is a protected species. Even if they weren't, their wings are mostly cartilage and provide little in the way of tender muscle. A good replacement is sole or halibut. These delicate, tender flatfish are readily available throughout the northern hemisphere.

4 filets of sole or halibut
1 teaspoon smoked sea salt
1 cup whole wheat flour
4 tablespoons unsalted butter
¼ cup chopped fresh sage
4 cups plain yogurt
2 tablespoons apple cider vinegar
½ cup capers

1. Season fish with salt, and then dredge in flour. Set aside for 15 minutes to let the flour absorb the moisture, which will make a crispier crust.

2. Heat butter in a large, heavy skillet over high heat. Add sage and cook until it wilts slightly. Add the fish, being careful not to crowd them (you may need to work in batches). Cook until browned on one side, 3 to 5 minutes. Flip and brown on the other side. Remove from the pan and keep warm.

3. In the same pan, add yogurt, vinegar and capers. Stir, scraping the cooked bits from the bottom of the pan. Reduce this mix by half. Season to taste. Plate the fried fish, garnish with additional sage if desired, and pour the pan sauce on top. Serve with crusty hunks of your preferred Northrend regional bread.

World of Warcraft

Bread of the Dead

Makes about 1 dozen

This holiday favorite is served throughout Azeroth during the Day of the Dead. Players must make it to receive an achievement and participate in the celebration of ancestors. If you are lucky enough to consume it, you'll experience a rise in stamina, strength, and agility for an hour. It may also unwittingly increase your waistline.

Grated zest of 1 large orange
¼ cup brandy, warmed
½ cup dried figs, chopped
½ cup dried peaches or apricots, chopped
½ cup dried dates, chopped
½ cup milk
¾ cup brown sugar
1¾ teaspoons (1 package) active dry yeast
⅓ cup olive oil
1 tablespoon ground cardamom
½ cup toasted pumpkin seeds (pepitas)
1½ teaspoons sea salt
3-4 cups all-purpose flour
1 egg, whisked

1. Combine the orange zest, brandy, and dried fruits in a bowl. Set aside to plump for 30 minutes (this can also be done overnight).

2. Combine milk, brown sugar, yeast, oil, cardamom, and pumpkin seeds in a separate bowl. Stir to dissolve. Let stand until foamy, about 10 minutes. Add salt, and then slowly stir in flour, ½ cup at a time, until a firm dough is formed. Turn out onto a floured surface. Knead for 8 to 10 minutes, until smooth and elastic, adding flour only as needed to control stickiness. Return the dough to the bowl, cover, and set aside to double in volume, about 1 hour.

3. Preheat oven to 375°F. Coat baking sheet with nonstick spray. Turn risen dough onto a floured surface. Divide into golf ball-size pieces. Roll each into a tight ball. Rest on the counter for 10 minutes, covered (this is called proofing).

4. Transfer balls to prepared pan. Brush with whisked egg, and using a sharp knife or scissors, slash or snip across the top of each roll to create a decorative mark that will help the dough expand in the oven. Bake until golden brown and hollow sounding when tapped on the bottom, 20 to 30 minutes. The dough should have an internal temperature of 210°F. Cool completely.

5
The Potterverse

Food plays an important role in the world of Harry Potter. A universe about a culture that spans centuries, set in the rich history of the British Isles, amidst a boarding school filled with hungry kids, is going to involve meals of some kind occasionally. But J. K. Rowling's meals don't simply fill our mind's bellies—they warm our hearts. In these novels, the food is delightful, comforting, evocative, and reflects a feeling of family and tradition.

In the beginning, the boy from under the stairs is welcomed to Hogwarts School of Witchcraft and Wizardry with a feast to fill his long-empty belly. The food is prepared in the kitchens of Hogwarts by house elves, originally brought to the school by one of its four founders, Helga Hufflepuff. The kitchen lies directly beneath the Great Hall, and the completed dishes—many of which are still prepared according to Helga Hufflepuff's original recipes—are placed on long tables in the kitchen, then magically transported to the Great Hall above.

While the house elves were brought to Hogwarts in an attempt to provide them with a safe, abuse-free environment, they were still enslaved. This becomes a point of contention between our heroes in *Harry Potter and the Goblet of Fire*, and it is just one example of the food in this series being used not simply as pretty window dressing, but as an important tool to illustrate the deeper issues we all face. These recipes have been chosen because they're iconic to the stories and representative of Great Britain, an island playing just as important a role as Harry Potter, Ron Weasley, and Hermione Granger. Its culinary traditions are unique, its tastes often acquired, and its customs delightful.

Steak and Kidney Pudding

Serves 6-8

Steak and kidney, a national dish in Britain, is referenced throughout the Potterverse. It's served at the Leaky Cauldron, opened in the sixteenth century by Daisy Dodderidge (who is found on a Chocolate Frog trading card). The Leaky Cauldron now appears to Muggles (those with no magical abilities) as an abandoned storefront near Charing Cross Station in London, but in preceding centuries, it welcomed all. A gateway between the Muggle and wizard worlds, it's the primary entrance to Diagon Alley, and a place where steak and kidney will always be a featured item. The dish has evolved since 1861, when it first appeared in *Mrs. Beeton's Book of Household Management* using merely steak, kidneys, salt, and pepper. Later versions saw the addition of other ingredients including mushrooms, onions, and even oysters. Both the pudding and pie versions are English traditions. This pudding is steamed in a bowl, rather than baked in a pan. If you dare to try it, I guarantee Daisy Dodderidge will smile at you from her collector's card.

FILLING

1 cup all-purpose flour
1 teaspoon sea salt
1 teaspoon cracked black pepper
1½ pounds chuck roast, flank steak, or skirt steak, diced
½ pound lamb kidneys, cleaned and diced
2 tablespoons vegetable oil
4 slices bacon, diced
2 medium yellow onions, diced
8 ounces mushrooms, sliced
1 tablespoon unsalted butter
½ cup Guinness dark ale or stout
2 cups beef stock
2 bay leaves
1 tablespoon Worcestershire sauce

PASTRY

2 cups all-purpose flour
1 teaspoon baking powder
2 teaspoons sea salt
½ cup beef suet or lard, chopped fine
4 tablespoons unsalted butter, plus 2-3 tablespoons extra for greasing
¼-½ cup cold water

Chopped parsley for serving

1. Generously butter a 1-quart ceramic or Pyrex bowl. Have ready a heavy Dutch oven with a tight-fitting lid big enough to fit the bowl inside. Make sure the lid seals tightly when the bowl is inside.

2. To make filling: Mix together flour, salt, and pepper. Toss diced beef in flour mixture and shake off excess. Set aside at room temperature. Repeat with diced kidney. Heat oil in a large heavy saucepan. Add diced bacon, onion, and mushroom. Cook, stirring over medium heat until fat is rendered and onions and mushrooms are golden. Remove bacon, onion, and mushroom with a slotted spoon. Set aside. Return pan to heat. Add butter. Working in batches, add enough floured beef cubes to cover bottom of pan, but don't crowd. Cook on high until browned. Remove from pan, set aside, and repeat with remaining diced beef, then kidneys. When meat is browned, return empty pan to heat. Deglaze with ale, scraping all crusty charred bits from the bottom. Add stock, meat, and mushroom mixture. Add bay leaves. Bring to a simmer. Cover. Cook on low heat for 1½ to 2 hours. Remove from heat. Season with Worcestershire, salt, and pepper. Cool completely while you prepare the pastry.

3. To make pastry: Combine flour, baking powder, salt, suet, and butter in a large bowl. Cut the fats into dry ingredients. Add ¼ cup cold water. Mix until a dough forms (add more water as necessary). Turn out onto a lightly floured surface. Knead 2 to 3 minutes until smooth. Set aside one-fourth of the dough. Roll out the remainder until it's large enough to line the bowl, with ½ inch extending over the lip.

4. Spoon in filling. Brush extended lip of dough with water. Roll remaining dough into a circle, place on top, and pinch to seal. Cover the bowl with buttered parchment paper, then again with foil. Bring a kettle of water to a boil. Place the bowl in the Dutch oven and fill the bottom with boiling water to reach three-fourths up the sides of the bowl, carefully pouring in between pudding bowl and Dutch oven. Cover with the lid. Place over low heat. Simmer 2 hours, adding more water as needed (check every ½ hour).

5. Remove the bowl from the Dutch oven and cool 10 minutes before turning out onto a serving platter. Top with chopped parsley.

Cornish Pasties. Savory Filling

Makes 10-12

Ron Weasley is frequently shoving food into his mouth. We get a vivid description of him scarfing pasties on the Hogwarts Express and during preparation for the third task of the Triwizard Tournament. They are a ubiquitous English snack.

Pasties have a special history in Cornwall. Consumed by nobles in the Middle Ages, the pasty was usurped by the working class in the seventeenth century and is associated with the mining tradition of southwest England. Pasties were chosen for their portability and ability to stay tasty all day. Many legends survive about this miner's lunch, including tossing a piece of crust down the mineshaft to placate the Knockers, mischievous leprechaun-like creatures. Though known to pull pranks and steal tools, Knockers also warned of collapse by knocking on the walls of the mine. This warning, likely the creaking of the earth as timbers gave way, was assured as long as the Knockers were kept happy with pasty crust.

A pasty can have a sweet or savory filling. Miners often took pasties filled with both to work—sweet on one end, meat on the other. Pumpkin pasties can be purchased at the Wizarding World of Harry Potter at Universal Parks & Resorts, but until you book your trip, you can make them yourself. Also, be careful to rhyme pasty with nasty, not tasty.

PASTRY

3 cups all-purpose flour
1 teaspoon sea salt
½ cup suet, lard, or unsalted butter, diced and chilled
1 egg
2 teaspoons white or cider vinegar
3-5 tablespoons water

SAVORY FILLING

(Dice all ingredients in a uniform size—1-inch cubes are preferred)
12 ounces cubed beef skirt steak or chunk steak
½ cup diced root vegetables-rutabagas (also known as swedes or neeps), parsnips, or turnips
½ cup diced onion
1 cup peeled and diced potatoes
1 tablespoon thyme
Pinch sea salt and pepper
2-3 tablespoons unsalted butter or clotted cream
1 egg, for wash

1. Combine flour and salt in a large bowl. Add fat, cutting it into flour until the mixture resembles rough cornmeal. Stir in egg and vinegar. Slowly add water, until the mixture comes together as dough. Form dough into a flat disk, wrap in plastic, and refrigerate at least 1 hour. Dough can be refrigerated for 2 days or frozen for several weeks.

2. For filling, combine everything but butter in a large bowl (meat goes in raw—it will cook in the oven). Toss. Moisten with a tablespoon or two of water. Set aside.

3. Preheat oven to 400°F. Line a baking sheet with parchment paper or coat lightly with nonstick spray. Dust work surface with flour. Pinch off as much dough as you'll need for one pasty (enough for an 8-inch circle). Knead briefly to soften slightly. Pat into a disk (start round, end round). Roll out into a circle about 8 inches in diameter and ¼-inch thick. Roll in one direction only; give the dough a quarter turn after each roll. Roll, turn, roll, and turn, until it's the size you need. This way, you will keep it roundish and will know instantly if it starts to stick, enabling you to compensate with a dusting of flour.

4. Place about ½ cup filling in the center of your circle. Top with a knob of butter or clotted cream. Fold one edge over to create a half moon. Seal edges with a crimp (traditional pasties have 17 to 24 crimps, but pressing tightly with a fork is acceptable). Place pasty on baking sheet. Repeat with remaining dough and filling. Miner's wives carved their husbands' initials into the edge of the dough as a steam vent—and to help differentiate them from those of their coworkers. Whisk the egg with a pinch of salt and a splash of water to create a wash, and then brush over each pasty.

5. Bake at 400°F for 20 minutes, until well browned. Reduce heat to 325°F. Continue cooking for another 20 to 30 minutes. Cool a bit before stuffing your face like Ron.

Cornish Pasties, Pumpkin Filling

Makes 10-12

The novels don't specify if the pumpkin pasties from Honydukes are sweet or savory. However, given the rest of the fare in that shop, we can assume it's sweet. That said, savory pumpkin pastries are found worldwide, such as Central Asian pumpkin bishak, Mexican pumpkin empanadas, and Italian pumpkin ravioli. So, here you will find two filling versions to try.

SWEET PUMPKIN FILLING

3 cups pumpkin puree (or one 15-ounce can)
3 tablespoons brown sugar
½ teaspoon each ground cinnamon, nutmeg, cardamom
½ teaspoon sea salt
Grated zest of ½ orange
2-3 tablespoons unsalted butter or clotted cream

SAVORY PUMPKIN FILLING

2 cups fresh pumpkin or butternut squash, diced in ½-1 inch cubes
1 clove garlic, minced
½ cup yellow onion, minced
¼ cup minced fresh sage (or ½ teaspoon dried)
½ cup grated Parmesan cheese (not Cornish, but it's good; use cheddar if striving for authenticity)
½ teaspoon sea salt
Pepper to taste
2-3 tablespoons unsalted butter or clotted cream

Prepare pastry as for Savory Filling (page 92). Mix ingredients for either recipe except butter. Assemble, adding a knob of butter to the center before sealing. Form and bake as earlier recipe.

Butterbeer

Makes 1 gallon

Butterbeer is the butterscotch-flavored beverage of choice in the village of Hogsmeade. It's said to have a slight alcoholic content, which hardly affects wizards but is known to get house elves very drunk. In the wizarding world, butterbeer takes the form of a caramel-y cream soda. This can easily be achieved at home by simply adding seltzer water to store-bought butterscotch or caramel syrup. But for those who strive for authenticity, homemade soda is the way to go.

When making soda, fermentation creates the carbonation. The bubbles are carbon dioxide, a byproduct of yeast feeding on carbohydrates (in the form of sugar in this case). There are two ways to achieve this. The easiest is to purchase champagne yeast, which is formulated for beverage fermentation, producing less gas than the yeast preferred in bread making. A slightly more advanced method—though not at all difficult—is to make a soda starter like the following. You'll need a couple of weeks, but it's the closest thing to real wizardry that you can do in your kitchen. No doubt this is the way the house elves do it.

SODA STARTER

Mason jar and lid, sterilized (run it through the dishwasher, or submerge for 10 minutes in boiling water)
1 large piece ginger, finely diced
7 to 8 tablespoons granulated sugar
2 cups filtered water
Cheesecloth
Rubber band

SODA SYRUP

2 cups organic cane sugar
1 cup brown sugar
1 gallon filtered water, divided
¼ teaspoon cider vinegar
½ teaspoon sea salt
1 vanilla bean, split
1-gallon jug
1 cup strained Soda Starter
Cheesecloth
Rubber band
Funnel
Bottles with tight seals

1. In the sterilized jar, combine 2 tablespoons of finely diced ginger, 2 tablespoons of sugar, and the water. Stir well to combine. Cover with cheesecloth, secure with a rubber band, and set aside on your kitchen counter at room temperature. Stir it again in 5 to 6 hours.

2. The next day, feed with an additional 1 tablespoon each chopped ginger and sugar. Stir well. Repeat feeding and stirring two or three times a day, every day for 5 to 7 days, keeping the jar at room temperature. When the starter begins to bubble and smell a bit yeasty, it's ready. Store in the refrigerator until ready to make your soda.

3. In a large saucepan, combine sugars, and enough of the filtered water to create a wet-sand consistency. Wash any excess sugar off the inside of the pot (to prevent crystallization) and bring it to boil over high heat (DO NOT STIR, as it increases the chance of crystallization—let the bubbles do the stirring). At the boil, add vinegar and salt. Cook until the sugar turns a deep amber caramel color, 5 to 8 minutes. Turn off the heat and immediately add 6 cups of filtered water. Add it carefully, but promptly. You want to stop the cooking process so the caramel doesn't burn, but you must also be careful that it doesn't erupt like lava. Scrape and add vanilla bean, then set aside at room temperature until cool.

4. When cool, remove vanilla bean, transfer to gallon jug, add Soda Starter and remaining water (leave a couple inches headroom). Mix well. Cover with cheesecloth. Secure with rubber band. Keep at room temperature for 3 to 5 days. Stir two or three times a day until you see signs of fermentation (bubbles). With funnel, transfer into clean, sterilized rubber gasket swing-top bottles, glass soda bottles with caps, or clean plastic bottles with screw caps. A tight seal is imperative to keep carbonation in the bottles. Leave at room temperature and test one bottle after 3 days. Open carefully (over a sink, in case of eruption) and check for carbonation. If you desire more bubbles, let the remaining bottles sit for a couple more days. When it is to your liking, refrigerate.

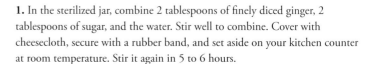

Mrs. Dursley's Violet Pudding

Serves 8-10

In *Harry Potter and the Chamber of Secrets*, the Dursley family throws a dinner party on Harry's birthday, but not in celebration of it. They're entertaining a potential business client and his wife. Mrs. Dursley proudly creates a pudding for the event, covered in a mountain of cream and sugared violets.

Although Petunia Dursley (née Evans) is a despised character because of how she treats Harry (boarding him under the stairs, making him do all the chores), the source of her wrath is heart-wrenching. The Evans family are Muggles, but Petunia's sister, Lily (Harry's mother), displays magical abilities. When Lily is accepted to Hogwarts, Petunia asks for admittance but is rejected. From then on, if she even acknowledges her sister, it is as a freak. Petunia meets Vernon Dursley, marries him, and has a son. When she finds her orphaned nephew, Harry, on their doorstep, she treats him poorly, but cares for him. She keeps the wizarding world secret, while still letting him return to her home every summer to recharge his family blood protections, keeping him safe from the dangerous Lord Voldemort.

Extravagant and decadent, yet suburban and ordinary, Mrs. Dursley's pudding is a perfect symbol for her longing to be accepted. Unfortunately, in an effort to get Harry expelled from Hogwarts (to protect him from an evil conspiracy), Dobby, a house elf, sends the pudding hovering through the air as the Dursleys entertain. Harry must use magic to prevent disruption of the party, resulting in a pudding catastrophe.

In the United Kingdom, the word *pudding* can be a term for any dessert. There are steamed puddings, baked puddings, sponge puddings, and puddings that look like flan. Christmas or figgy pudding is a fruit-filled holiday tradition. Blancmange is a gelatinized pudding flavored with almond. There are also savory puddings, like Yorkshire, blood pudding and haggis, and of course, steak and kidney pudding. Fans who have tried to recreate Mrs. Dursley's pudding often interpret it as a layer cake or a trifle. But in the film, the dessert more closely resembles a vacherin, recreated here, which is traditionally comprised of meringue, cream, fruit, and buttercream. It's an extraordinary dessert for your ordinary dinner party.

MERINGUE

1 cup egg whites
(about 8 eggs; reserve the
yolks for the buttercream)
1 teaspoon sea salt
1½ cups granulated sugar

1. Draw four 8-inch circles on parchment paper (many salad or dessert plates are this size). Place the paper onto baking sheets, with the drawings side down. The lines should be visible through the underside of the paper. Spray the paper (not the side with marks) lightly with nonstick spray.

2. Combine egg whites, salt, and granulated sugar in a large heat-resistant bowl and stir. Place the bowl over a pan of barely steaming water (bain-marie) that is smaller in diameter than the bowl, so that the bowl does not touch the bottom of the pan or the water. Stir continuously, but slowly, until the egg whites have warmed and the sugar has dissolved, about 3 minutes. Transfer to a stand mixer, or use a hand mixer, to whip on high speed until stiff peaks form and the whites are cooled.

3. Divide the meringue among the 4 circles, and spread evenly to create 4 meringue disks of about ½-inch thick. Let these sit in the open air while you preheat the oven to 150°F. (This resting period allows a skin to form on the meringue that prevents cracking during baking.)

4. Bake meringues until firm and dry, anywhere from 1 to 4 hours, depending on your oven (smaller ovens cook them faster). If the meringues begin to brown,

open the oven door slightly, and continue to bake until firm and crisp. Alternatively, dry the meringue in a dehydrator for 8 to 10 hours on low. This method is ideal, because it doesn't require monitoring and always results in white meringue. Set meringues aside in a cool, dry place (not the refrigerator, as it is full of moisture that will render your meringues soggy) until you're ready to assemble the dessert.

MOUSSE

4 ounces white chocolate chips (it's okay to eyeball this, about half an 8-ounce bag)
2 cups heavy cream
1 tablespoon granulated sugar
1 teaspoon sea salt
1-2 tablespoons rose water
½ cup red currant, raspberry, or strawberry jam

1. Place white chocolate chips in a large bowl and set aside. Combine cream, granulated sugar, and salt in a saucepan. Place over high heat. Stirring occasionally, bring the cream to a boil. Pour immediately over the chocolate, and let sit undisturbed for 5 minutes.

2. Add rose water and jam to the chocolate. Whisk to a smooth, creamy texture. Place in the refrigerator. Cool completely, until it reaches a spreadable consistency, about 1 hour. Keep refrigerated until ready to assemble the dessert.

BUTTERCREAM

8 egg yolks
1 teaspoon sea salt
1½ cups granulated sugar
2½ cups (5 sticks, 1 pound 4 ounces) unsalted butter, at room temperature
½ cup red currant, raspberry, or strawberry jam

1. Combine egg yolks, salt, and granulated sugar in a large heat-resistant bowl. Stir together. Place over a pan of steaming water (bain-marie) that is smaller in diameter than the bowl, so that the bowl does not touch the bottom of the pan, or the water. Stir continuously, but slowly, until the egg yolks have warmed and the sugar has dissolved, about 3 minutes. Transfer to a stand mixer, or use a hand mixer, and whip on high speed until a cool ribbon has formed (a ribbon is when the mixture turns pale yellow, thickens, and has doubled in volume).

2. Continue whipping on high. Add butter 1 tablespoon at a time, continuously, not too fast or slow, but at a measured pace. When all the butter is in, whip until mixture comes together in a homogenous, creamy texture. (It may look like cottage cheese for a while. This is normal, and it will come together once it is sufficiently emulsified.) When the buttercream is smooth and homogenous, fold in the jam by hand. Cover and reserve at room temperature until you're ready to assemble the dessert.

CRÈME FRAÎCHE

You can buy readymade crème fraîche, and sweeten slightly, or make this mock version.

1 cup heavy cream
1 cup sour cream
2 tablespoons granulated sugar
1 teaspoon vanilla extract
½ cup red currant, raspberry, or strawberry jam

1. Combine heavy cream, sour cream, granulated sugar, and vanilla in the bowl of a stand mixer, or use a handheld mixer and a large bowl, and whip on high speed until thickened to medium peaks. Fold jam in at the end and keep refrigerated until you're ready to assemble the dessert.

CANDIED VIOLETS

Candied violets are a French staple decoration and can be bought in fine bakery supply stores. You can also make them yourself.

Clean flower petals (use violets, roses, or any edible flower untreated by pesticides)
1 egg white
Pinch sea salt
2 cups superfine sugar (you can make your own by pulsing granulated sugar in a food processor)

1. Separate petals and wash gently (with a water spray bottle), then gently pat them dry with a paper towel. Line a baking sheet with parchment paper.

2. Whisk egg white and salt together until frothy. Dip each petal in the foamy egg white. Dab off excess with a paper towel. Generously dredge each egg-dipped petal in sugar and place on the prepared baking sheet to air-dry. Allow to sit at room temperature until each petal becomes crisp, about 1 hour. Set aside until you're ready to decorate your dessert.

ASSEMBLY
Place one meringue disk on your serving platter. Spread on a generous layer of white chocolate mousse. Top with a second meringue disk. Spread this layer with buttercream. Top with a third meringue disk. Spread this layer with two-thirds of the crème fraîche. Cover with final meringue disk. Finish with the remaining crème fraîche. Decorate with candied violets, fresh berries, or cherries. Refrigerate until ready to serve (keep out of reach of the house elf).

Chocolate Frogs

Makes about 2 dozen

Honeydukes, the famous sweet shop in Hogsmeade, maintains a trolley on the Hogwarts Express, from which travelers can purchase treats. It is here, on his first trip to Hogwarts, that Harry is introduced to all manner of magical goodies, which he purchases and shares with his new friends. It's a delightful scene, not just because it is introducing us to our heroes, and them to each other, but also because it perfectly encapsulates the joys of youth. All of life's adventures ahead in the great unknown: new friends, a super-cool train, and a boatload of sweets. We can all delight in the wonder of the boy who never had friends until now, let alone magical candy that jumps out of his hand.

Chocolate frogs are frog-shaped bonbons made with a high percentage of Croakoa that makes them act like real frogs, and tucked in their boxes are collectible cards of famous witches and wizards. Chocolate frogs make reoccurring appearances, as Christmas gifts, rewards, and to cheer up friends laid up in Hogwarts' infirmary. They come in both dark- and white-chocolate varieties, which no doubt inspired the popular wizard game in which a variety are let loose and the players try to grab only the dark ones.

If you have a frog-shaped mold, a chocolate frog is as easy as pouring in melted chocolate and letting them chill. But for a more flavorful treat, try the following recipe. They will not hop, or, for that matter, look like real frogs, but they are much tastier.

4 cups rolled oats
1 cup granulated sugar
¼ cup brown sugar
½ cup cocoa powder
1 cup (2 sticks, 8 ounces) unsalted butter, at room temperature
2 tablespoons coffee or brandy
1 teaspoon ground cardamom
½ vanilla bean, split and scraped
½ cup chocolate chips (or chopped fine chocolate of your choice)
1 cup shredded coconut

1. In a large bowl, combine oats, sugars, and cocoa. Add butter, and use a handheld mixer to cream together into a dough (or use a stand mixer).

2. In a microwave or over a double boiler (bain-marie), combine coffee, cardamom, vanilla bean seeds, and chocolate chips. Melt, stirring until smooth. Add to the oat mixture and blend well.

3. Spread coconut out on a large plate. Pinch off walnut-size pieces of dough, roll into balls, and then dredge in coconut to cover thoroughly. Your frogs are ready to eat, or you can store them in the fridge. If you really want to delight your guests, serve them with homemade wizard cards.

Treacle Tart

Serves 6-8

Treacle tart is Harry's favorite. He loves it so much, he smells it when he falls under the influence of Amortentia, the world's most powerful love potion. Treacle is the sticky, gooey British equivalent to molasses, available in golden and black grades. Golden syrup has a buttery rich flavor, used in baking and much like honey as a condiment on toast. Black treacle is akin to blackstrap molasses, with a slightly bitter taste. If you can't get golden syrup, light molasses will suffice. For the breadcrumbs, I prefer using plain white bread, letting it dry and stale for a day, then pulsing it in a food processor. If you purchase breadcrumbs, make sure they are not seasoned.

PASTRY

1 pound unsalted butter
1 cup sugar
½ teaspoon sea salt
1 teaspoon vanilla extract
3¼ cups cake flour
Dried beans or rice

FILLING

2 tablespoons unsalted butter
1 cup golden syrup or light molasses
6 tablespoons plain white bread crumbs
3 tablespoons heavy cream
1 egg
Grated zest of 1 lemon

TOPPING

1 cup heavy cream
1 tablespoon sugar
1 teaspoon vanilla extract

1. Pastry: Combine butter and sugar in a large bowl and cream together until smooth. Add salt and vanilla, then flour. Stir together until a dough forms. Press into a flat disk, wrap, and refrigerate for at least 1 hour.

2. Filling: Combine butter with the syrup in a small saucepan, and warm over medium heat until loose. Remove from heat. Stir in breadcrumbs, cream, egg, and lemon zest. Set aside to cool.

3. Preheat oven to 375° F. Coat a 9-inch removable-bottom tart pan with non-stick spray. Dust work surface with flour. Knead dough briefly to soften, pat into a disk (start round, end round). Roll out a circle a couple inches larger than your tart pan and about ¼-inch thick. (Roll in one direction only, then give dough a quarter turn after each roll. Roll, turn, roll, turn, until it's the size you need. This way, you keep it roundish, and you'll know instantly if it starts to stick, enabling you to compensate with a dusting of flour.) Line tart pan with dough, pressing it into place. Pinch off top flush with the rim of the pan. If the dough cracks or tears, just patch it as needed. When your shell is lined, freeze it for 10 minutes.

4. Blind bake your crust. Take the dough shell out of the freezer, line it with foil, and fill it to the rim with dried beans or rice (this is a fake filling to simulate the weight of a real filling that holds the dough in place as it bakes). Cook until the rim begins to turn golden brown, about 20 minutes. Spin it around occasionally, so it browns evenly. When it looks to have solidified, very carefully remove the fake filling and liner. Return it to the oven to bake until the bottom is golden brown, and clearly cooked. Remove the shell carefully from the oven and let it cool.

5. Pour cooled treacle filling into your blind-baked shell, return to the oven for 30 to 40 minutes, and bake until the filling has just set. (If you feel ambitious, you can weave a lattice made of extra pastry for the top of your tart. Brush the lattice with egg wash before baking, for a nice golden brown.) Remove from oven. Cool slightly.

6. Topping: Whip cream, sugar, and vanilla to stiff peaks. Serve slices of warm tart with a dollop of whipped cream and a side of Amortentia potion.

6
The Jedi

"Well, the Force is what gives a Jedi his power. It's an energy field created by all living things. It surrounds us and penetrates us; it binds the galaxy together."—Obi-Wan Kenobi

Telekinesis, mind control, clairvoyance, and a ghostly afterlife may seem magical, but Jedi aren't wizards or sorcerers. They don't use potions or spells. They don't fly on broomsticks or shoot sparks from a wand. As anyone who knows *Star Wars* can tell you, they use the Force. In more than forty years since George Lucas created *Star Wars*, the Force has connected the Star Wars universe, exploring what was, in the 1970s, referred to as New Age ideas about God. Lucas introduced the idea of a metaphysical power that understands and communicates with the living world in an unseen way. With it, he sets up a classic struggle between good and evil. There are those who wield power selflessly and those who use it selfishly. The dark side of the Force is harnessed by the Sith, who use it aggressively. The Jedi practice the light side for defense and peace.

Some characters have a deeper connection to the Force than others, explained by the presence of midi-chlorians, a microscopic, intelligent life-form in the cells of all living organisms. More midi-chlorians means a greater potential to use the Force. Anakin Skywalker (aka Darth Vader, or the Chosen One) has the highest midi-chlorian count in galactic history. George Lucas once compared the use of the Force to yoga—everyone can do it, but only a few truly master its power.

Kyber Crystal Cocktail

Serves 2

The Jedi Order was founded thousands of years before the rise of the Galactic Empire ("A long time ago in a galaxy far, far away") to protect devotion to the light side of the Force. The Jedi have Force affinity and are required to follow certain principles—self-discipline, patience, public service, and ethics—that becomes known as the Jedi Code. Their role is primarily diplomatic, but their mastery of the Force occasionally requires them to wield a deadly weapon, the lightsaber.

Jedi younglings are Force-sensitive children identified at birth. After initial training, they participate in the Gathering ritual to seek out a kyber crystal, a naturally occurring element that is able to focus and direct the energy of the Force. The crystals are chosen, meditated upon to imbue them with the light side of the Force, and then used to construct the Jedi's lightsaber.

Further training between Jedi Masters and Padawan learners include the Jedi Trials, a series of tests in teamwork, isolation, fear, anger, betrayal, focus, instinct, and forgiveness. Upon successful passage, a Padawan learner is given the status of Jedi Knight and is then capable of performing solo missions for the Galactic Republic (later the New Republic).

Kyber crystals create lightsaber beams in colors related to the Force of the owner. Those who practice the dark side of the Force create a red-colored crystal, while the light side typically renders blue, green, or purple. This recipe is from the light side, and specifically references Jedi Master Yoda, because he is awesome. He is also a vegetarian, hence the use of aromatic herbs. Also paying homage to the Jedi Order is the use of Chartreuse liqueur, which has been made by a monastic order since the seventeenth century.

1½ ounces gin
1½ ounces green Chartreuse liqueur
1 ounce sweet vermouth
Dash rose water
Fresh herbs for garnish

1. Combine ingredients in a large glass with ice or in a cocktail shaker. Stir or shake thoroughly, then strain between two coupe or rocks cocktail glasses. Serve with a garnish of fresh herbs.

Dagobah Root Leaf Stew

Serves 4-6

Jedi lore recounts the story of a rogue Jedi who searches for power and knowledge through the dark side of the Force and develops a following, known as the Sith. A civil war erupts, and after years of fighting, the Sith begin to turn on one another, allowing the Jedi to defeat them. This brings peace to the galaxy and leads to the creation of the Galactic Republic. The Jedi serve as the Republic's peacekeeping force for over one thousand years, and during that era, the leader of the order is Yoda, the Grand Master Jedi.

Some Sith survive, regroup, and wait to exact revenge. When conflicts arise between Republic member worlds, the Jedi are reluctant to raise an army, and miss both the infiltration of the Sith into the Republic Senate (Senator Palpatine) and the recruitment of the Chosen One (Anakin Skywalker, aka Darth Vader) to the Dark Side. When the Jedi younglings are purged and Senator Palpatine seizes power of the Senate, Yoda realizes his failure and steals away to a remote planet of Dagobah. But Yoda's self-imposed exile isn't just penance for his hubris. Dagobah—the uninhabited, swampy, jungle planet— is strong with the Force and provides the perfect place to reconnect with the living elements of it.

Luke Skywalker arrives on Dagobah at the request of ghost Jedi Obi-Wan Kenobi, who comes in a vision while Luke is stranded in a snowstorm on the planet Hoth. "You will go to the Dagobah system. There you will learn from Yoda, the Jedi Master who instructed me." Luke is taken to Yoda's hut and fed this vegan stew made from galla seeds, mushroom spores, sohli bark, and Yoda's main source of food, yarum seeds. Since yarum cultivation is rare on Earth, try using dried mung beans or lentils instead.

1 large eggplant or 2 slender
Chinese eggplant, peeled and diced
¼ cup sea salt
½ cup dried mung beans or lentils
¼ cup olive oil, divided
2 tomatoes, chopped
1 pint cremini mushrooms, chopped
4 green onions, chopped
3 cloves garlic, minced
¼ cup mint leaves, chopped
1 tablespoon ground turmeric
1 teaspoon ground cumin
¼ teaspoon cayenne (or to taste)
½ cup grated parsnip
½ cup grated carrot
½ cup Italian parsley
½ cup chopped Thai
or Italian basil leaves
½ cup cilantro
1 tablespoon honey
Dollop plain yogurt
Crackers for serving, if desired

1. Sprinkle diced eggplant liberally with salt, toss to coat, and set in a colander to extract moisture. Drain for 1 hour.

2. In a small saucepan, cover mung beans with 2 inches of water and bring to a boil. At the boil, reduce heat. Simmer, stirring occasionally, until tender, 10 to 20 minutes. Drain.

3. Preheat oven to 350°F. Coat an oven-proof casserole with 1 to 2 tablespoons of the olive oil. Layer (one ingredient at a time) tomatoes, mushrooms, green onions, garlic, and mint on bottom. Sprinkle evenly with turmeric, cumin, and cayenne. Rinse the eggplant thoroughly to remove salt, and layer atop vegetables. Layer (again, one ingredient at a time) mung beans, parsnip, carrot, parsley, basil, and cilantro. Top with remaining 2 to 3 tablespoons olive oil and honey. Cover tightly. Roast for 1½ hours, or until bubbly, thick, and fragrant. Before serving, stir to mix ingredients and season to taste. Serve warm, with a dollop of plain yogurt and a crumble of crackers, if desired.

Jedi Ration Bars
Serves 6-8

Ration bars are emergency food rations, like today's power bars, carried by Clone Troopers during the Clone Wars, by Imperial Stormtroopers, and were part of X-Wing starfighter survival kits. Almost anything that flies—starfighters, gunboats, freighters, and escape pods—carried survival kits. In addition to ration bars, kits contained a thermal cloak, survival knife, distress beacon, glow rod, and medpac.

Having crashed on Dagobah, Luke nibbles his ration bar, as he and R2-D2 sort through their surviving equipment. It's here Luke meets Yoda, before the Jedi Master's identity is revealed. To test Luke's patience, Yoda is annoying, playing the doddering, ignorant fool and getting his curious hands into all of Luke's stuff, including the ration bars, which don't impress him.

But others in the *Star Wars* universe like them. Ewoks, the short, furry, stone-age inhabitants of the forest moon of Endor, appear to enjoy them. Princess Leia Organa used them to win over the first jittery Ewok she met, and who later helps her defeat a couple of Stormtroopers. Like Earth survival foods, these bars are loaded with protein-packed nuts and sweet, chewy fruit. They can be formed into any shape, but they fit best into your survival kit in the stick shape.

1 cup pitted dates
1 cup golden raisins
1 cup dried figs
3 cups boiling water
1 cup whole skin-on almonds
½ cup shredded coconut
¼ teaspoon ground cinnamon
¼ teaspoon ground nutmeg
Pinch of sea salt
1-2 cups whole wheat flour
1 cup cocoa powder

1. Combine dates, raisins, and figs in a large bowl. Cover with boiling water. Set aside for 15 minutes to soften, then drain completely and pat dry. Do not soak longer than this, as the moisture will make the bars too wet: 15 minutes is just enough time to make the fruit easier to grind.

2. In food processor, pulse drained dried fruits, processing to a sticky paste (it should form a ball in the processor). Add almonds, coconut, cinnamon, nutmeg, and salt. Continue to process until nuts are finely chopped and everything is well mixed. Add flour 1 tablespoon at a time, until the mixture becomes firm and doughlike and can be easily formed into a rope.

3. Turn dough out onto a clean surface. Working in batches, roll into ropes about 1-inch thick. Cut into logs 2 to 3 inches long. Roll in cocoa powder to thoroughly coat. Place in airtight container and chill for 2 to 3 hours or overnight to firm up.

VARIATIONS
Other ingredients that Stormtroopers can fold into their processed paste include seeds (sesame, pumpkin, poppy, sunflower), other types of nuts, chocolate chips, or M&M's.

Mos Eis-Tea

Makes about 1 gallon

"You will never find a more wretched hive of scum and villainy"—Obi-Wan Kenobi

We encounter the spaceport town of Mos Eisley on the planet of Tatooine after Obi-Wan and Luke Skywalker discover the murdered bodies of Luke's family. They decide to head out in search of Princess Leia Organa, whose holographic message they find inside the droid R2-D2. They need a pilot, and Mos Eisley is the most likely place for them to find one. Indeed, they find Han Solo there.

Tatooine, as a whole, is a pretty unpleasant planet. Covered in sand dunes, heated by two suns, with no water source and no vegetation, Tatooine supports life only because of moisture farmers like Luke's uncle Owen, who harvested water out of the air. The Jawas and Tusken Raiders are the only native inhabitants, but the population rises when mining deposits are discovered. It is the home planet of both Anakin and Luke Skywalker, and it is the headquarters of Jabba the Hutt.

Mos Eisley is larger than it appears on-screen, because a good portion lays underground, shielding residents from the desert heat. Though Luke was raised on Tatooine, our first view of Mos Eisley is also his. You can still see it today, as the sets used to film exterior shots are still in Tunisia, which has developed into a popular *Star Wars* tourist destination.

This recipe is meant to quench your own hive of villainy. It makes a gallon of refreshing "tea" (perfect for a party), but it can be adjusted by reducing all measurements equally. Please don't drink any before jumping behind the wheel of your speeder.

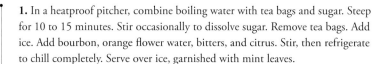

4 cups boiling water
4 black tea bags (try Darjeeling, Assam, or Ceylon)
2 cups sugar
4 cups ice
4 cups bourbon
2 tablespoons orange flower water
2 tablespoons orange bitters
Grated zest and juice of 1 orange
Grated zest and juice of 1 lime
Mint leaves for garnish

1. In a heatproof pitcher, combine boiling water with tea bags and sugar. Steep for 10 to 15 minutes. Stir occasionally to dissolve sugar. Remove tea bags. Add ice. Add bourbon, orange flower water, bitters, and citrus. Stir, then refrigerate to chill completely. Serve over ice, garnished with mint leaves.

VARIATION
For a nonalcoholic version, replace bourbon with half orange juice and half apple juice.

Cantina Cocktail Snack Mix

Serves 6-8

Chalmun's Cantina (known also as the Mos Eisley Cantina) is the hangout of star pilots visiting Tatooine. It's remembered for its many exotic alien patrons and for the swinging jatz jizz tunes of Figrin D'an and the Modal Nodes (who entertain the crowds regularly as a means of paying off a gambling debt). It is also where Luke and Obi-Wan first meet Han Solo and Chewbacca.

First built by pioneers as refuge against Tusken Raiders, the cantina has been a brewery, monastery, boarding house, armory, and illegal spice den. A wookiee named Chalmun eventually purchases it and converts it into a tavern. One reason for the popularity of the cantina is Chalmun's droid detector, which screens out Imperial security droids sent to eavesdrop on private conversations.

This snack, with its mix of salty and sweet, is a great accompaniment to any galactic beverage and makes great snacking while you watch your favorite *Star Wars* movie.

1 cup pecan halves
1 cup walnut halves
1 cup peanuts
1 cup almonds
2 tablespoons unsalted butter
½ cup brown sugar
1 teaspoon sea salt, divided
Pinch black pepper
Pinch white pepper
Pinch crushed red pepper flakes
Grated zest of 1 orange
1 tablespoon minced fresh rosemary
1 cup golden raisins
2 cups air-popped popcorn

1. Preheat oven to 350°F. Spread nuts on a dry baking sheet. Toast for 5 to10 minutes. Stir, and toast for another 5 to 10 minutes, until nuts are golden and fragrant.

2. Melt butter in large sauté pan over medium. Add brown sugar, ½ teaspoon salt, black pepper, white pepper, red pepper flakes, orange zest, and rosemary. Add raisins, toss in butter to moisten. Add nuts, toss over medium heat until sugar is dissolved and nuts are well coated. Add popped corn, toss again. Immediately pour out on to a baking sheet or parchment paper. Add remaining salt. Cool to room temperature before serving. Store in an airtight container.

Alderaan Gorak Roasted in Malla Petals

Serves 4

In the first *Star Wars* movie, we learn that the planet Alderaan is home to Princess Leia Organa, who asks Obi-Wan Kenobi for help via a hologram stored in R2-D2. In that film, the First Galactic Empire's planet-killing Death Star destroys the planet in an attempt to instill fear. However, as the saga expands (in prequel films, television series, and the numerous canon novels that explore the backstories of the initial characters), we learn more and more about the beautiful home of Princess Leia.

During the early days of the rebellion against the Galactic Empire, Alderaan was considered a safe world and was known galaxywide as "the planet of beauty." It was famous for its flora and fauna, natural landmarks, snow-capped mountains, wide oceans, and vast green valleys. Its cities were carefully designed to respect that natural environment.

Found only on Alderaan, the Gorak bird was considered a delicacy. The closest way to approximate it on Earth is to use the Chinese silk chicken (aka Silkie), an ornamental breed named for its furry, satiny plumage, its bluish-black skin, flesh and bones, its five toes and blue earlobes. They are commonly available in Asian markets, or, if you are not fortunate enough to have a similar shopping mecca in your vicinity, you can use chicken or duck. The other Alderaanian ingredient is the malla plant, similar to our own daylilies, which are also used frequently in Chinese cuisine and can be easily found in dried form.

1 Chinese silk chicken,
neck and innards removed
(or regular chicken or duck)
One ½-inch piece ginger, grated
4 cloves garlic, minced
2 tablespoons soy sauce
1 teaspoon sesame oil
1 tablespoon hoisin sauce
3 cups dried lily buds
2 yellow onions, sliced
3 cups shiitake mushrooms, sliced
2 large carrots, sliced
Grated zest and juice of 1 orange
Pinch of salt
2 tablespoons black sesame seeds

1. Rinse the chicken inside and out and pat dry. Place it in a bowl or zip-top bag with ginger, garlic, soy sauce, sesame oil, and hoisin sauce. Toss to coat, then set aside in the refrigerator to marinate for 6 to 8 hours, or overnight.

2. To prepare lily buds, rinse off any dirt, then cover with boiling water. Set aside to rehydrate for 1 to 2 hours. When buds are very soft, drain off water, reserving it for the final roasting. Trim off the tough end of the softened lilies and slice in half lengthwise.

3. Preheat oven to 475°F. Line a large roasting pan with onions, mushrooms, carrot, orange zest and juice, prepared lilies, and lily water, strained of sediment. Place the marinated chicken on top, skin-side up. Sprinkle with salt. Roast for 20 to 30 minutes, until the skin is crispy and the meat is medium-rare (165°F on a meat thermometer). Rest the bird for 5 minutes before slicing. Serve on a bed of mushroom-onion-lily mixture, sprinkled with black sesame seeds.

Canto Bight Clams Casino

Makes 2 dozen

Canto Bight is a coastal city on the desert planet Cantonica. Like Las Vegas or Monte Carlo, Canto Bight is filled with casinos and racetracks, making it the preferred destination of the rich and famous (or those trying to be). We are introduced to this den of greed in *Star Wars: The Last Jedi* when the characters Finn (FN-2187) and Rose Tico search for the Master Codebreaker to help disable the dictatorial First Order's hyperspace tracker. Like other gambling towns, there is an undeniable air of luxury, demonstrated by flowing bubbly and swanky snacks, including this classic hors d'oeuvre.

2 dozen littleneck clams
8 slices bacon, diced
1 cup breadcrumbs (panko is preferred, but not a necessity)
½ teaspoon sea salt
½ teaspoon cracked black pepper
½ cup (1 stick, 4 ounces) unsalted butter
3 Italian sausages, casings removed
½ red onion, minced
4 green onions, minced
3 cloves garlic, minced
Grated zest and juice of 1 lemon
¼ cup white wine
¼ cup Italian parsley, chopped
¼ cup mint leaves, chopped
2-3 cups rock salt

1. To clean clams, first remove the sand by submerging in cold, salted water, and then set aside for 30 minutes. Remove from water and scrub shells.

2. Meanwhile, sauté bacon in a heavy skillet, stirring, until the fat is rendered and the meat is crispy. Add the breadcrumbs and continue to cook and stir to coat evenly, until breadcrumbs are toasted, about 4 to 5 minutes. Remove from heat, season with salt and pepper, and set aside to cool.

3. In same pan, melt butter. Add sausage, breaking it up into small bits as it cooks. Add red and green onions and cook until translucent, 5 to 6 minutes. Add garlic, lemon zest and lemon juice. Continue to cook until golden. Add wine and prepared clams. Cover. Simmer until clams open, about 3 to 6 minutes, checking frequently, removing them as they open. Set aside opened clams to cool. Continue to cook sausage and onions until caramelized and liquid has evaporated. Set aside to cool. When cool, stir in parsley and mint.

4. Open the clams, separating the shells and freeing each clam. Line a baking sheet with rock salt. Nestle the bottom shells into the salt, then place one clam back in each shell. Top each clam with the sausage and onions, then a generous sprinkling of bacon and breadcrumb mixture. Clams can be prepared to this point up to a day ahead and stored in the refrigerator.

5. Preheat oven to 450°F. Place baking sheet in oven and cook to heat through, about 5 minutes. Carefully transfer to dish and serve immediately.

Blue Milk Pudding

Serves 4

Blue milk, or Bantha milk, is a staple on Outer Rim planets, including Luke Skywalker's home planet of Tatooine, where we first encountered it on the table of Aunt Beru and Uncle Owen. Referenced occasionally in a number of *Star Wars* video games as a slang term, "blue milk run" means a simple mission. It's the product of the female Bantha, a large hairy mammal with huge spiral horns, ridden by Tusken Raiders. Bantha are prized for their milk, hide, and meat. Known for its sweet flavor and rich texture, blue milk is used for yogurt, ice cream, cheese, and this pudding. The otherworldly texture of blue milk pudding can be approximated on Earth by using arrowroot as a thickener.

3½ cups whole milk
1 teaspoon freshly ground cardamom
1 teaspoon rose water
Pinch sea salt
1 or 2 drops blue food coloring
⅓ cup arrowroot
½ cup sugar
1 cup blueberries or blackberries

1. In a heavy-bottomed saucepan, combine milk, cardamom, rose water, and salt. Bring to a boil. At the boil, remove from heat, stir in food coloring, and let stand for 10 minutes.

2. In a large bowl, whisk together arrowroot and sugar, then slowly stir into warm milk. Return to the stove. Warm gently, stirring, until mixture thickens, about 3 to 5 minutes. Be careful not to scorch. Strain into serving dishes. Chill until set, 1 to 2 hours, or overnight. Serve topped with berries.

7
Grimm's Fairy Tales

Once upon a time, there were two German brothers, Jakob and Wilhelm Grimm, in what was then the Holy Roman Empire. Meanwhile, the Napoleonic Wars were raging, and their country fell to the French. The people resented everything French, and searched for ways to emphasize their German identity. This prompted the brothers to study and compile Germanic stories.

By the time the Brothers Grimm were writing in the late eighteenth century, fairy tale collections were not new. What set the brothers apart was their attempt to collect German folk tales as a means of nationalistic propaganda, to bring the culture together and preserve traditions, with their first edition of *Grimm's Fairy Tales* published in 1821 as entertainment for adults.

Because the first reviews of the book were critical, the brothers decided to gear it toward children. They removed sexual references, changed wicked mothers into stepmothers (keeping motherhood sacred), and enhanced its Christian references. But they did not remove the violence, especially with regards to punishment of evil. The tales have taken on a life of their own over the years, being tweaked and sanitized by subsequent authors and filmmakers, surviving into the modern era.

"Hansel and Gretel"

Golden Gingerbread with Lemon Curd

Serves 8-10

This story, about parents abandoning children to avoid feeding them, likely grew out of a real episode in the history of Europe, the Great Famine of 1315-1317. A change in the western European climate led to dramatically decreased agricultural output, and by 1317, famine affected all levels of society. (It was this famine that dramatically increased the effects of the subsequent Black Death, also known as the Great Plague, of 1347-1351.) Seed grain and working animals were eaten, children were abandoned, and tales of cannibalism were rampant. It is from here that we get the tale of "Hansel and Gretel," whose parents abandon them in the woods during a time of hunger, leaving them to the devices of an old woman who wants to eat them.

The story details a witch who entices the children to a house built of bread covered with cakes. It does not reference a gingerbread house specifically, but gingerbread enjoyed wide popularity by this time. During the Middle Ages, the spice trade popularized exotic flavors, and lebkuchen, a German spiced honey cake, was a favorite. The tradition spread to England, where in the sixteenth century, Queen Elizabeth I enjoyed gilded versions in the shapes of her courtiers. At the same time, witches were accused of using gingerbread men in "image magic." The practice of gingerbread house construction began in the early 1800s, around the same time as the Grimm's first edition was printed. This version is not for construction, but for snacking. The addition of lemon is a seventeenth-century tradition, in the form of a thin lemon glaze. Here, this flavor pairing is interpreted with a creamy lemon curd.

GINGERBREAD

3 cups all-purpose flour
2 teaspoons baking powder
2 tablespoons ground ginger
1 teaspoon ground nutmeg
1 teaspoon ground cardamom
Pinch ground clove
½ teaspoon sea salt
2 teaspoons molasses
1 cup milk
1 cup (2 sticks, 8 ounces) unsalted butter
2 cups brown sugar
4 large eggs

LEMON CURD

1 cup granulated sugar
Grated zest of 2 lemons
1 cup lemon juice
3 tablespoons unsalted butter
3 eggs
Powdered sugar for serving

1. Preheat oven to 350°F. Coat a 9 x 13-inch baking pan with nonstick spray. In a large bowl, combine flour, baking powder, spices, and salt. Whisk to combine, and set aside. Stir together molasses and milk in a separate bowl, and set aside.

2. In a stand mixer or large bowl with hand mixer, cream together butter and brown sugar until smooth and lump free. Add eggs one at a time, mixing each in thoroughly. Alternate adding flour and milk mixtures in three increments, making sure each addition is well mixed. Transfer batter to the prepared pan and bake for 20 to 30 minutes, until firm to the touch and a toothpick inserted in the center comes out clean. Cool to room temperature.

3. For lemon curd: Combine granulated sugar, lemon zest and juice, butter, and eggs in a small, heavy-bottomed saucepan. Heat, stirring constantly, until thick, about 5 minutes. Strain. Set aside to cool with plastic wrap pressed directly on the surface, to prevent a skin from forming. To serve, cut cake into squares, top with a spread of curd and a dusting of powdered sugar if you like.

Rampion Salad

Serves 4-6

The name Rapunzel comes from a bellflower known as the rampion, eaten throughout Europe as both a leafy vegetable and a root. The Grimm story was based on earlier tales published in the seventeenth century by Italian and French poets, who named their long-haired beauty Persinette, or Petrosinella (meaning parsley)—irrefutable evidence of the story's connection to salad.

As the story goes, a couple live next to a witch, who has a garden. The pregnant wife gets a craving for rampion, and so the dutiful husband breaks into the garden to satisfy her. The wife eats her rampion salad and begs for more. When the witch catches the husband stealing, he begs for mercy. She allows him to take all the rampion in exchange for the baby. The couple agrees.

The witch names the girl Rapunzel (after the stolen herb) and raises her as her own. The girl grows beautiful, with long, golden hair. To keep her as a companion forever, the witch locks her in a tower in the woods. With no door or staircase, the only way for the witch to visit Rapunzel is to climb up her hair, which she calls forth with the well-known "Rapunzel, Rapunzel, let down your hair, so that I may climb the golden stair."

A prince comes across the tower, hears the girl singing, and witnesses the witch climbing up the hair ladder. When the witch departs, he climbs up, and he and Rapunzel fall in love. In the first Grimm edition, the illicit visits are discovered when the naive girl wonders aloud to her witch-mother why her dresses are getting tighter. The Brothers Grimm scrapped the theme of premarital sex, and unplanned pregnancy, in the second edition.

Rapunzel is punished with a haircut, and banished to the desert, where she gives birth to twins. The prince, meanwhile, discovers Rapunzel's absence on his nightly visit and gets shoved (or suicidally jumps) out of the tower, landing in a briar patch, which blinds him. He wanders in the dark for years until he hears Rapunzel's voice. His eyesight is restored by her magical tears, and the family lives happily ever after.

2 cups baby spinach leaves
2 cups dandelion greens or arugula
2 cups curly kale
2 cups grated rainbow carrots
4 slices bacon, diced
½ cup chopped hazelnuts
⅓ cup brown sugar
⅓ cup red wine vinegar
1 tablespoon Dijon mustard
Pinch sea salt
¼ teaspoon cracked black pepper
½ cup edible flowers, such as marigold, borage, chive, and nasturtium

1. Thoroughly wash and dry all greens. Toss them together with the carrots in a salad bowl and set aside.

2. In a large, heavy skillet, cook bacon until the fat is rendered and meat is crispy. Add hazelnuts and continue to cook until toasted. Remove from heat. Whisk in brown sugar, vinegar, and mustard. Season with salt and pepper. Toss over greens. Serve immediately, garnished with edible flowers.

"Cinderella"

French Pumpkin Gratin

Serves 4-6

The tale of a persecuted heroine such as Cinderella is an ancient one. The first one to lose a shoe was Rhodopis, a Greek slave girl whose sandal is snatched by an eagle before she gets to marry the king of Egypt. The ninth-century Chinese story of Ye Xian also recounts a lost shoe, as well as a cruel stepmother. Several tales in the *1,001 Arabian Nights* also recount evil siblings. But it is the early European versions from the seventeenth century that are the closest to modern interpretations, placing our heroine amongst cinders as a servant girl. These were also the first to incorporate the help of a magical godmother, mice turning into footmen, and pumpkins turning into coaches.

In the Grimm version, Aschenputtel (Ashfool) loses her mother to the plague, and her father remarries. Her stepsisters banish her to the kitchen, steal her clothes, give her rags to wear, and make messes for her to clean. Yet Aschenputtel remains good, praying at her mother's grave regularly for better circumstances, joined by a bird in whom she confides. When a local prince holds a three-day festival to find a bride, Aschenputtel's stepmother only allows her to attend if she cleans up the lentils tossed on the floor, which she does with help from her bird friends. Still not allowed to go, she heads to her mother's grave, where the birds present her with a beautiful dress and shoes. At the festival, the prince falls for her, and they dance all night. But at the end of the night, Aschenputtel flees. After two nights of this, the prince has the stairs covered in pitch (something like tar). Again she runs, but loses one shoe on the sticky stairs.

The prince goes looking for the girl that fits the shoe and arrives at the house. The first stepsister, urged by her mother to make the shoe fit, cuts off her toes. This works, until the prince notices the blood (the birds point it out). He tries the second stepsister, who cuts off her heel. He falls for it again, and the birds set him straight once more. He finally gets to Aschenputtel, who fits the shoe perfectly, with no blood, and they live happily ever after. Later editions add in a wedding, during which the birds peck out the eyes of the stepsisters. While this tale is captivatingly gory, it is a French version from which most of the modern themes emerge—a glass slipper, a godmother, and a pumpkin. This recipe is dedicated to the transformation of produce into a mode of transportation, arguably the most endearing feature of this story. Certainly it is the least bloody.

1 small pumpkin or butternut squash, peeled and thinly sliced

3 russet potatoes, peeled and thinly sliced

1 yellow onion, peeled and thinly sliced

½ teaspoon sea salt

¼ teaspoon cracked black pepper

4 tablespoons unsalted butter

2 shallots, diced

1 clove garlic, minced

2 sprigs fresh thyme

3 or 4 fresh sage leaves

4 tablespoons all-purpose flour

2¼ cups milk

2 cups shredded Gruyere cheese

½ teaspoon freshly grated nutmeg

2-3 amaretti cookies, crumbled

1. Preheat oven to 400°F. Coat a 1-quart casserole dish with nonstick spray. Layer pumpkin, potatoes, and onions alternately in prepared casserole. Season with salt and pepper. Set aside.

2. Melt butter in a large skillet over high heat. Add shallot, garlic, thyme, and sage. Sauté until golden. Add flour. Stir to create a roux. Slowly add milk and continue cooking until thick. Remove from heat. Stir in cheese and nutmeg until melted. Pour over layered pumpkin and potatoes. Cover with foil. Bake for 45 to 60 minutes, until tender. Remove foil for the last 5 minutes, to brown the top. Sprinkle amaretti cookie crumbs over the top and serve.

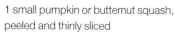

Roasted Pork with Poison Apple Chutney

Serves 4-6

The Grimm's tale of "Schneewittchen" ("Snow White") contains many elements that we recognize today, such as a magic mirror, dwarves, and a poison apple. But it is missing the one element that modern audiences expect: love's first kiss. No kisses here. In the story, a queen has a daughter whom she names after blood she once saw dripping on snow. When the queen died, the king remarried a beautiful but vain woman who practiced witchcraft with a magic mirror that never lied. When the mirror eventually decrees that Snow White is the fairest, the witch becomes envious. She orders a huntsman to take Snow White into the forest, kill her, and return with her lungs and liver. He can't do it, however, instead bringing back the lungs and liver of a boar as proof (she'll never know the difference). The witch fries it up and has it for lunch.

Snow White ends up at the home of seven dwarves, who let her stay as a housekeeper. The witch figures this all out, and takes matters into her own hands. Disguised as a peddler, she appears at the home of the dwarves, selling a fancy laced corset. Snow White tries it on, and the queen laces it up so tightly that Snow White faints. The dwarves arrive just in time to revive her, so the witch tries again, this time with a poisoned comb. Oblivious, Snow White combs her hair, but is saved by the dwarves once again. Finally, the witch tries a poisoned apple. This works, and the dwarves place her in a glass casket.

A prince comes across the glass casket in the forest and is smitten (with a corpse). The dwarves agree to let the prince take the casket. As it is being moved, one of the servants trips, drops the casket, and dislodges the poisoned apple from Snow White's throat. She wakes up and marries the prince. Everyone is invited to the wedding, including the witch. When her identity is revealed, the prince orders her to wear red-hot iron shoes and dance herself to death. No kiss. Just some necrophilia and torture.

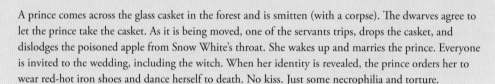

½ cup raisins
½ cup currants
6 cups cold water, divided
¼ cup salt
1½- to 2-pound pork tenderloin
2 Fuji or similar apples, cored and sliced into wedges
1 yellow onion, sliced
3 cloves garlic
2 tablespoons olive oil
2 tablespoons brown sugar
1 tablespoon Dijon mustard
1 teaspoon cayenne pepper
1 teaspoon cracked black pepper
1 teaspoon cracked pink peppercorns
1 teaspoon dried thyme

1. Combine raisins, currants and 2 cups of the water. Set aside at room temperature to plump. Combine remaining 4 cups water and salt in a separate bowl. Stir to dissolve. In a bowl, submerge pork in the brine and refrigerate for 4 to 6 hours, or overnight. (This brine will help keep the finished roast moist.)

2. Preheat oven to 425°F. Drain raisins and currants, place in a bowl, and add apples, onion, and garlic cloves. Drizzle with oil, toss, and spread out on a heavy-bottomed roasting pan. Rinse brined pork, lay it on top of the apples, and tuck the thin end under, so that the loin has a uniform thickness.

3. In a small bowl, stir together brown sugar, mustard, peppers, and thyme. Rub across top of loin. Roast for 25 to 30 minutes, until the internal temperature reaches 145°F on a meat thermometer. Remove from the oven and rest for 5 minutes before slicing thinly. Serve with a generous spoonful of the pan chutney.

Cuisses de Grenouilles à la Provence

Serves 4-6

Like "Snow White," Grimm's "The Frog Prince" is also missing the true love kiss. As a young princess tosses her golden ball near a well, it slips through her fingers and rolls into the water. She cries but is interrupted by a talking frog (a prince who has been put under a spell). He offers to retrieve the ball if she promises to be his friend. Frogs are gross, but she really wants that ball, so she agrees. However, once she has her hand on the ball, she quickly forgets her promise. So, the frog stalks her.

Back at the palace, it's dinnertime, and there's a knock at the door. The princess opens it to find the frog, reminding her of the promise. She shuts the door, but her father, the king, insists that promises must be kept. Disgusted, she lets the frog in. He eats next to her and sleeps with her on her pillow. When she awakes next to a slimy frog, she hurls it across the room in disgust. It smacks against the wall and explodes his frog guts. But that breaks the spell, and he becomes a handsome prince, whom she agrees to marry. In some versions, the frog transforms after merely sleeping on her pillow. It is not until a much later version that we get the kiss. In all versions, the frog is described as an annoying, disgusting creature—although I would argue that the spoiled princess is the more annoying of the two.

Frog's legs are a historically French dish, but are given a decidedly Cajun feel here. They are not a common feature at most supermarket meat counters, but are readily available in the freezer section of Asian markets.

2 cups buttermilk
6 cloves garlic, minced, divided
6 pairs frog's legs
2 cups all-purpose flour
1 tablespoon dried thyme
Vegetable oil for frying
1 teaspoon sea salt
4 tablespoons unsalted butter
2 shallots, minced
Grated zest and juice of 1 lemon
1 large bunch Italian parsley, chopped
½ teaspoon cracked black pepper

1. Combine the buttermilk and half the garlic in a large bowl. Add the frog's legs and toss so they are well coated. Refrigerate for at least 2 hours, or overnight if possible.

2. Strain the frog's legs out of the buttermilk, and let sit in a colander for a few minutes to dry. Mix together flour and thyme. Add the legs and toss to coat thoroughly. Let sit at room temperature while you prepare for frying.

3. Heat 2-3 inches of oil in large heavy-bottomed skillet. When the temperature reaches 350°F, add a batch of frog's legs. Don't crowd them in the pan. Fry until golden brown, about 2 to 3 minutes per side, then remove to a paper towel-lined platter. Keep warm. Repeat with remaining legs. Sprinkle with salt.

4. Melt butter in a large skillet over high heat. Let the butter begin to brown before carefully adding remaining garlic and shallots (it may splatter a bit). Remove from heat and add lemon zest, juice, and parsley. Add fried frog's legs back to the pan, toss to coat, then serve, sprinkled with salt and black pepper.

8
Magical Nannies

Nannies are some of the most enduring characters in storytelling. In *The Sound of Music*, governess Maria tames the von Trapp children with her skills as a songstress and a seamstress. In the *Eloise* books, it's Nanny who keeps everything in check. In *Peter Pan*, it's Nana, who, despite being a dog, cares for the Darling children. And in *Harriet the Spy*, it's her nanny, Ole Golly, who's encouraging of Harriet's interests.

Being a kid is hard, especially for children with indifferent, overwhelmed, or absent parents. These situations call for a Magical Nanny who can fix problems and help parents discover what their job really is. She gets to the heart of problems, frames the ideal family dynamic, and brings out the best in everyone. She's fun loving, encouraging individuality, or strict, providing boundaries. Either way, Magical Nannies have a deep, heartwarming effect on the entire family.

In nineteenth-century Europe, women in the upper echelons of society employed servants to assist with child-rearing tasks. Enter the nanny—occupying a space between servant and family—not quiet either, but fulfilling the functions of both. The Magical Nanny infused children's literature with a figure recognized by many British families, so she's almost always British. In the early decades of the twentieth century, the United States didn't possess the same level of aristocracy as England, so similar American stories revolve around teachers, neighbors, adoptive parents, or grannies. Nevertheless, the story of the alternative parent offering stability is a childhood favorite.

We Are Not a Codfish and Chips

Serves 4

P. L. Travers created the character of Mary Poppins in a series of books, the first of which was published in 1934. Most know her from the Disney film that, surprisingly, almost didn't happen. In 1938, after learning that *Mary Poppins* was his daughter's favorite book, Walt Disney tried to purchase the rights, but Travers was reluctant. She finally relented in 1961, with script-approval rights.

The film, *Mary Poppins*, opened in 1964 to great acclaim, except from Travers. Of her complaints, the worst was Disney's representation of Mary as pretty, not stern, as originally created. Disney made her more magical, subtracted two children from the Banks family, and gave them an Edwardian mansion, rather than the original ramshackle house. Disney also gave the ditzy Mrs. Banks the suffragette movement as an excuse for her distracted parenting.

Despite her reaction, Travers became a wealthy woman thanks to the film, and she continued to write about Mary into the 1980s. As for the rest of us, the movie is much beloved, with subsequent television, radio, and theater productions, and even a Russian version of the film. And it brought Mary Poppins to an audience that would otherwise never have known her.

There are many iconic images from the film *Mary Poppins*—a magic compass to travel around the world, an upside-down tea party, an enchanted merry-go-round—but it's her unique way with words that is most endearing. "Spit spot!" "Well begun is half done." And, when the children are stunned, their mouths agape, "We are not a codfish." Open up your mouth for this classic British tradition of fried fish and potatoes, in homage to this excellent admonishment.

½ cup all-purpose flour, divided
¼ cup cornstarch
1 teaspoon baking powder
1 teaspoon sea salt, plus more for seasoning
½ teaspoon cracked black pepper
⅓ cup Guinness stout
⅓ cup seltzer water
4 russet potatoes
4 large (5- to 6-ounce) cod fillets
2-3 cups vegetable oil for frying
Malt vinegar, for serving

1. In a large bowl, mix together ¼ cup of the flour, cornstarch, baking powder, salt, and pepper. Add stout and seltzer water. Stir until thick and smooth. Refrigerate for 30 minutes.

2. Meanwhile, slice potatoes into wedges, about ½-inch thick. Place in a saucepan, cover with cold water, and bring to a boil. Reduce heat. Simmer for 5 minutes. Drain, pat dry with paper towels, and refrigerate.

3. Toss cod fillets with remaining flour and set aside to dry. Heat oil in a heavy deep skillet to 350°F. Add the potatoes in batches (do not crowd). Cook for 3 to 4 minutes to blanch (not to brown). Remove with a slotted spoon and drain on paper towels.

4. Dip floured fish in the prepared batter and place carefully into the oil. Fry in batches—do not crowd the pan—until golden brown and crisp on all sides, 5 to 8 minutes. Remove to drain on paper towels.

5. Increase oil temperature to 400°F. Fry the potatoes a second time, until golden brown and crisp, about 5 minutes. Season with salt. Serve hot, with the fish and a shaker of malt vinegar.

Toad in the Hole

Serves 4-6

This Disney film, released in 1971, was based on the 1943 book, *The Magic Bed Knob: or How to Become a Witch in Ten Easy Lessons*, and its 1947 sequel, *Bonfires and Broomsticks*, by Mary Norton. It takes place during World War II, following Carrie, Charlie, and Paul Rawlins, evacuated from London during the Blitz. They're placed in the care of Miss Eglantine Price, who's preoccupied with a witch correspondence course and keeps them quiet with time travel on a magical bed. The film focuses on the quest for the Substitutiary Locomotion spell that can bring inanimate objects to life, as they travel to places inhabited with animated characters. They find the spell and use it to bring antique armor to life—and defeat the Nazis.

Miss Price's lack of childcare knowledge becomes apparent when she tries to feed them cabbage buds, rose hips, elm bark, and stewed nettles. They request English classics, including this recipe, Toad in the Hole, sometimes interpreted as a sausage baked into a roll. The more traditional preparation is this one, surrounded with fluffy, eggy Yorkshire pudding.

YORKSHIRE PUDDING

⅞ cup all-purpose flour
½ teaspoon sea salt
2 eggs
½ cup milk
½ cup water
3-4 tablespoons bacon fat, lard, or butter
8 sausages (British bangers if possible), precooked and sliced (if using popover or muffin pan) or whole (if using a skillet)

ONION GRAVY

2 tablespoons vegetable oil
2 yellow onions, sliced
1 cup red wine
3 tablespoons unsalted butter
3 tablespoons all-purpose flour
2 cups beef broth
1 teaspoon soy sauce
1 teaspoon Worcestershire sauce
½ teaspoon sea salt
Pinch white pepper

1. Sift together flour and salt in a medium bowl. In a second bowl, whisk together eggs, milk, and water until frothy. Add the dry ingredients to the wet and stir together until just incorporated. Refrigerate for 1 hour, then remove and allow the batter to come back up to room temperature.

2. Preheat oven to 400°F. Place a cast-iron popover pan, muffin pan, or skillet into the oven, and preheat for 10 minutes. When very hot, carefully add a dab of fat or butter to each popover cup (or skillet). Next, carefully add 2 or 3 slices of sausage to each cup (or place whole sausages into the large skillet). Next, add the pudding batter on top of the sausages (half full for popover cups or half full for skillet). Bake for 20 minutes at 400°F. Reduce heat to 350°F and cook for 10 to 25 minutes longer, until well risen and golden brown.

3. Meanwhile, make the onion gravy. In a second pan, add oil and onions. Cook until translucent. Reduce heat, add wine, cover, and cook for 10 to 15 minutes, or until very soft. Increase heat, and reduce liquid to 1 tablespoon. Add butter. When melted, add flour, and whisk to create a roux. Slowly add beef broth, mixing continuously, to create smooth gravy. Season with the remaining ingredients. Serve hot popover toads, covered in warm onion gravy.

Food Fight Wedding Cupcakes

Makes 1 dozen

Nanny McPhee is often compared to Mary Poppins, but they're on opposite ends of the nanny spectrum. Nurse Matilda (as McPhee is known in the original books) isn't opposed to using chaos to get her job done. She arrives when she's needed the most, following a long line of nannies terrorized by the Brown children. But this nanny is a witch, and she uses magic outright to make bad children behave. Thumping her walking stick on the floor produces a spell that forces the children to continue to misbehave until they beg for release (for instance, a child faking illness ends up in the hospital). It's a taste-of-your-own-medicine approach, rather than a spoonful of sugar.

The *Nurse Matilda* books, created by Christianna Brand, were published in a series, starting in 1964. They inspired the 2005 film *Nanny McPhee*, which used the character's last name to avoid confusion with the 1996 film, *Matilda*, based on the Roald Dahl novel. The theme of *Nanny McPhee* is teaching proper behavior. As with *Mary Poppins*, the film takes liberties with the original. Mr. Brown is portrayed not as part of an inept couple, but as an overwhelmed widower. To keep the family fortune, he gets engaged to a wicked woman. To save their father and themselves from this evil stepmother, the children pretend to be swarmed by bees at the wedding, resulting in a pastry-based food fight. The beauty of the scene is in the choice of green and pink wedding colors. Recreate the scene yourself with the following recipe (though it would be a shame to waste these beautiful cupcakes in a food fight). Follow the film's color scheme or create your own.

BUTTERMILK CAKES

1½ cups cake or all-purpose flour
2 teaspoons baking powder
½ teaspoon sea salt
1 cup buttermilk
Grated zest of 1 orange
1 teaspoon orange flower water
3 eggs
1⅓ cups sugar
½ cup vegetable oil
Assorted food coloring

BUTTERCREAM FROSTING

1 cup egg whites
1½ cups sugar
Pinch sea salt
4½ sticks (18 ounces) unsalted butter, softened
½ teaspoon vanilla extract
Assorted food coloring

1. To make the cakes: Preheat oven to 375°F. Coat a muffin tin with nonstick spray, then insert muffin liners and coat them with nonstick spray too. In a large bowl, sift together flour, baking powder, and salt. Set aside. In a separate bowl, combine buttermilk, orange zest, orange flower water, eggs, sugar, and oil. Stir the wet ingredients into the dry and mix to thoroughly combine.

2. Divide batter evenly into two bowls. Add food coloring to each (your color choice), starting with a single drop, mix, and increase as desired. (It's easier to add color, but you can't subtract it.) Layer batter colors randomly into prepared muffin tins, filling each about ¾ full. Bake 15 to 20 minutes, until firm and a toothpick comes out clean. Remove from pan. Cool completely.

3. To make the frosting: Bring a medium pot of water to a boil. In the bowl of a stand mixer, or using a handheld mixer, combine egg whites, sugar, and salt. Whisk briefly. Place over the steaming water. Turn off heat. Gently stir until egg whites are warmed and sugar is dissolved (check this by dipping your clean finger in). Remove from the pan of water. Whip vigorously, on high speed of the electric mixer, until cool and at stiff peaks. Slowly but steadily, add chunks of butter while whipping. When all the butter is incorporated, whip for another 2 to 3 minutes, until the mixture has a smooth, fluffy, frosting texture. Keep at room temperature until ready to use.

4. Divide frosting between 2 to 4 small bowls (for as many colors as you like), adding food coloring to each. Plop several colors by spoonful into a piping bag, careful not to mix them. Decorate cupcakes as desired. Chill until ready to serve.

Traditional English Crumpets

Makes 8-12

The 1970 cancellation of the television series *The Flying Nun* left an open spot in the ABC prime-time lineup. The most popular shows at the time were *Bewitched* and *I Dream of Jeannie*. In an attempt to capture a similar audience, the sitcom *Nanny and the Professor* was created. It centers on the family of widowed professor Harold Everett and his three children, Hal, Butch, and Prudence. The professor is quite unable to manage his kids, and so, out of nowhere, Phoebe Figalilly (also known as Nanny) appears at his doorstep, just when he needs her most. She is dressed in an Inverness cape and cap (very much like those of Sherlock Holmes) and is very British. Despite her lack of references, the professor hires her on the spot. At first, the children are befuddled by her strange nature. But eventually, they warm to her, and she brings a sense of order to the chaotic household.

We never learn exactly what Nanny is, but she always seems to know what is going to happen just before it does. This fascinates the children and keeps them on their toes. Occasionally, it is proposed that Nanny is not really human and has lived for several centuries. Her quirkiness manifests not only in her wardrobe, but also in the Ford Model A she drives, with a radio that only plays stations from the 1930s (another mystery). She never hides her clairvoyance (or whatever it is), even from the nosy neighbors, and thus hilarity ensues.

Nanny and the Professor ran for three seasons. Though initially placed between *The Brady Bunch* and *The Partridge Family*, it was moved from time slot to time slot, and lost its audience. The star, Juliet Mills, was a Shakespearean actress from a theatrical family (daughter of actor Sir John Mills, sister of actress Hayley Mills). Pay homage to this British actor, in this very British role, with this recipe for crumpets. Similar in form and flavor to English muffins, crumpets are typically thinner and are traditionally never split when eaten.

1½ cups water
1 cup milk
Pinch granulated sugar
1 tablespoon active dry yeast
2 tablespoons unsalted butter, melted and cooled
3½ cups all-purpose flour
1 teaspoon baking powder
1 teaspoon sea salt

1. In a large bowl of a stand mixer, combine water, milk, sugar, and yeast. Mix together. Let stand for 5 minutes, until bubbly. Stir in butter, flour, baking powder, and salt. Beat for 2 to 3 minutes, then cover the bowl with a warm, moist towel. Set aside to rise for 1 hour, until expanded and bubbly.

2. Preheat griddle on medium. Generously coat inside of English muffin rings (or clean tuna cans with bottoms removed) with nonstick spray and set them on griddle. Pour about ¼ cup of batter into each ring. Cook for 3 minutes, until sides begin to solidify. Remove rings. Continue cooking until bubbles appear on the surface, another 2 to 3 minutes. Flip. Cook the second side for 2 to 3 minutes, until both sides are golden brown (watch the heat of your griddle and adjust accordingly, so as not to brown too quickly or too slowly). Set aside to cool and repeat with remaining batter. Toast. Serve with butter and jam.

Sugar Cookie, Peppermint, and Tea Ice Cream

Serves 4-6

This series of four books, begun in 1947 by author Betty MacDonald, tells the story of Mrs. Piggle-Wiggle, a widow who lived in an upside-down house that always smelled like cookies, in a neighborhood of misbehaving kids. Subsequent books were added to the series by her daughter, Anne MacDonald Canham, and Ann M. Martin, who is better known for her *Baby-Sitters Club* series.

Mrs. Piggle-Wiggle was in possession of a treasure chest, left to her by her late pirate husband. The chest contained all sorts of magical cures, which she administered to the neighborhood children on behalf of their parents, who could not get them to behave with the standard scolding, spanking, and yelling. Using tricks, magical powders, tonics, as well as treats (such as magic cookies that force kids to keep promises), she cures messy rooms, unwillingness to share, refusal to bathe, interrupting, lying, and other bad behavior. Her cures often follow the taste-of-your-own-medicine theory of discipline. A child refusing to bathe is caked with dirt that sprouts vegetables. Those who interrupt or gossip lose their voices. She uses many other clever tactics, like turning chores into a competition and curing boredom with a treasure hunt. She also gets help from farm animals demonstrating proper etiquette and hygiene.

Cookies and peppermints are a favorite of Mrs. Piggle-Wiggle. They're paired here with cambric tea, a weak tea with milk and sugar given to children at bedtime in the nineteenth century. Folded into easy, no-churn ice cream, it's sure to elicit the best behavior.

1 cup milk
2 bags English breakfast tea
One 13-ounce can sweetened condensed milk
1 teaspoon vanilla extract
1 tablespoon lemon juice
½ teaspoon sea salt
1 cup crumbled sugar cookies
½ cup peppermint candies, crushed
2 cups heavy cream

1. In a small pot, warm the milk, and then add the tea bags. Steep for 10 minutes, then discard the bags and cool the milk completely.

2. When cool, stir in sweetened condensed milk, vanilla, lemon juice, and salt. In a separate bowl, mix together cookies and peppermint bits.

3. In a separate bowl, whip heavy cream until it reaches soft peaks. Fold the cream gently into the tea-milk mixture. Transfer to freezable container, filling it halfway. Add half the cookies and candies in an even layer. Pile on remaining cream mixture. Finish with a layer of cookies and candies. Cover with plastic wrap, pressed directly onto the surface of the custard as much as possible (this prevents ice crystals from forming). Place in the freezer for about 6 hours, until firm and scoopable (thinner layers freeze faster)!

VARIATIONS
Chocolate: Omit the tea and add 1½ cups chocolate chips to the warming milk, stirring until completely melted.
Mix-ins: Use other types of cookies, candies, nuts, or fruits.
Fruity: Make a plain vanilla base (omit the tea). Before folding in the whipped cream, fold in about 1 cup of your favorite fruit puree or jam.

9

Disney Magic

Literal magic—witches, wizards, dragons, curses, spells—are a common feature in Disney movies. But it is the figurative magic that sets Disney apart from other studios. Stories that deliver courage, optimism, hope, adventure, friendship, and love continue to touch hearts all over the world. The magic of Disney also lies in its ability to delight adults. As grown-ups, we view the heroes with new appreciation because we have encountered many villains in our day-to-day lives. The added bonus of adult humor also makes for quality family viewing, which was Walt Disney's initial goal—strengthening the family.

Snow White, the first cel-animated full-length feature musical film (based on the Grimm's fairy tale) premiered in 1937. It employed 750 artists who produced two million sketches and 250,000 drawings. It was the first feature film to use the multiplane camera, which photographed multiple images at once, producing a greater sense of depth. It was also the first film of any kind to record and sell the soundtrack to the public. As with all his projects, Walt Disney used the most talented animators, composers, musicians, and actors. He was known to have spared no expense to provide what they needed to succeed, from live animal and human models to formal art training and research trips abroad. This, combined with the good-hearted, empathetic story material, proved a perfect recipe for Disney magic.

"The Sorcerer's Apprentice"

Butterfly Cake

Serves 10-12

In 1930, Disney began combining music and images in short animations titled the *Silly Symphony* series. These shorts were precursors to the film *Fantasia*. The most famous segment in the film, "The Sorcerer's Apprentice," is based on a German poem written in 1797 by Johann Wolfgang von Goethe, which was in turn inspiration for a symphonic poem by French composer Paul Dukas. Disney's original idea was to present the story and music in an animated short, with Mickey Mouse playing the apprentice. But a short would never earn back the expensive production costs, which led to the concept of a feature film comprised of separate animated musical numbers. With the working title *The Concert Feature*, artists like the conductor Leopold Stokowski and classical music aficionado Deems Taylor began considering songs to be included. The film premiered in 1940 with the title *Fantasia*, the first feature film of its kind.

When "The Sorcerer's Apprentice" begins, the sorcerer conjures a bat, which he then transforms into a butterfly. Recreate that transformation with this magical cake. It's an easy project, starting with one simple, round cake.

CAKE

3 cups cake flour
1 tablespoon baking powder
1 teaspoon sea salt
1 cup milk
2 teaspoons vanilla extract
Grated zest of 1 orange
2 cups granulated sugar
1 cup (2 sticks, 8 ounces) unsalted butter
4 eggs

FROSTING

2 cups powdered sugar
¾ cup (1½ sticks, 6 ounces) unsalted butter
¾ cup milk
½ teaspoon sea salt
1 teaspoon orange flower water
Food coloring, as desired
Assorted candies, dragées, shredded coconut, and sprinkles, as desired
Candy bar (optional)

1. To make the cake: Preheat oven to 350°F. Coat a 9-inch round baking pan with nonstick spray. In a bowl, whisk together flour, baking powder, and salt. Set aside. Combine milk and vanilla. Set aside. Combine orange zest and granulated sugar in a food processor or coffee mill. Pulse until sugar turns orange and fragrant.

2. Cream together butter and orange sugar until smooth and lump free. Add eggs, one at a time and mix thoroughly. Add the dry ingredients, alternating with the milk mixture, in three increments. Transfer to prepared pan. Bake for 25 to 30 minutes, until the top is firm and a toothpick inserted comes out clean. Cool for 10 minutes, and then invert onto a baking rack to cool completely.

3. To make the frosting: In a stand mixer, or in a bowl with a handheld mixer, combine powdered sugar and butter. Beat until smooth and lump free. Slowly add milk and continue beating until fluffy. Mix in salt and orange flower water.

4. To assemble the cake, first turn it upside down so that the flat side faces up. Working on your final serving platter, cut through the center of the cake, first in half—creating two semicircles, then at 4:00 and 8:00, so that the incisions resemble a peace sign. Separate the semicircles, and rearrange them with flat edges touching, curved-side out. Finally, open up the small triangular peace-sign sections to create the bottom butterfly wings up against the bottom of the upper wings. Adjust as you see fit for your butterfly.

5. Using an offset spatula, first spread a thin layer of frosting all over the cake. This is called a crumb coat and will make the final decorating easier. Color the remaining frosting as desired and use it to frost the butterfly's wings. Use candies, dragées, shredded coconut, and/or sprinkles to add dimension and detail. You can pipe the body of the butterfly with another color of frosting or insert a candy bar.

Mickey's Parmesan Broomsticks

Makes about 2 dozen

"The Sorcerer's Apprentice" recounts an episode in which an apprentice gets hold of his master's power but misuses it. In Disney's version, the sorcerer took off his hat and left his workshop. Mickey donned the master's hat and used its magic (which he was ill-equipped to handle) to enchant a broom to do his chore of fetching water to fill a well. But the well quickly overflowed, and Mickey realized he did not know the spell to stop it. He split the broom with an axe, but each piece became a whole broom, which continued fetching water. As the room flooded, and all hope was lost, the sorcerer returned and broke the spell. It's a classic tale of a smug learner overestimating his abilities and losing control. The first viewing of this scene can be scary for kids. Ease the tension with these cheesy hors d'oeuvres. Be sure to see the variations for alternative broom flavors.

½ teaspoon sea salt
½ teaspoon paprika
½ teaspoon dried oregano
½ cup finely grated Parmesan cheese
1 egg yolk
1 teaspoon water
1 package frozen puff pastry,
defrosted overnight
in the refrigerator

1. Preheat oven to 475°F. Line a baking sheet with parchment paper. Combine salt, paprika, oregano, and Parmesan in a small dish. Mix thoroughly. Whisk the egg yolk with a tiny pinch of salt and cold water.

2. Dust your work surface lightly with flour and unroll the puff pastry. Cut the dough into 1 x 6-inch strips. Use a pastry brush to coat each pastry strip with the egg wash on one side only. Sprinkle each one with the spice mix. Return to the refrigerator for 10 minutes. It is important to keep the dough cold during this next stage (refrigerate or freeze as needed to keep the dough easy to handle).

3. Twist each strip gently into a corkscrew-like shape. Place on the prepared baking sheet. Having the egg and spices on only one side accentuates the twist effect. Bake for 10 to 15 minutes, until golden brown and puffed. Rotate the pan periodically for even browning. Cool completely before serving.

VARIATIONS
Seeds: Replace paprika and oregano with poppy, sesame, sunflower, or chia seeds.
Pepper: Replace paprika and oregano with a mix of freshly cracked black, pink, or green peppercorns. Or spice it up with the addition of red pepper flakes.
Herbs: Replace paprika and oregano with freshly minced rosemary, thyme, tarragon, or mint.
Tomato: Replace egg wash with a mix of 3 tablespoons tomato paste or puréed sundried tomatoes and 1 tablespoon olive oil. Brush over pastry strips. Sprinkle with minced fresh herbs.
Sweet: Replace the paprika, oregano, and cheese with a mix of sugar spiced with either cinnamon, nutmeg, clove, allspice, cardamom, or a mixture.

Snow Eggs (Œufs à la Neige)

Serves 6-8

As early as 1937, Disney explored the possibility of a Hans Christian Andersen biography, including stories such as "Thumbelina," "The Little Mermaid," and "The Snow Queen." The idea went into development but experienced difficulties that included story issues, a devastating labor union strike, and World War II. So the Hans Christian Andersen project was shelved. In the late 1990s, after the success of *The Little Mermaid*, development for "The Snow Queen" resumed. But the Snow Queen as a villain was deemed unrelatable to today's audiences. Finally, the story was reimagined as *Frozen*, with sisters, a family dynamic that resonated with audiences. Elsa was no longer a villain, but a scared girl trying to cope with life—something everyone could relate to.

Celebrate your sister (or your queen) with snow eggs, also known as floating islands. This classic dessert involves three of the most important techniques a pastry chef must learn—whipping meringue, stovetop custard, and caramelized sugar. You might feel intimidated by this, but just, "let it go!" You can do this!

CRÈME ANGLAISE (VANILLA CUSTARD SAUCE)

2 cups milk
½ cup sugar
½ vanilla bean, scraped
8 egg yolks

MERINGUE

8 egg whites
⅓ cup sugar
Pinch sea salt

CARAMEL

¾ cup sugar
¼ cup water
Juice of ½ lemon

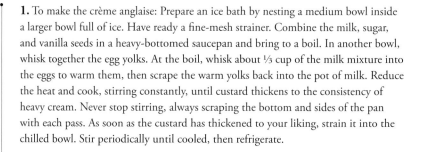

1. To make the crème anglaise: Prepare an ice bath by nesting a medium bowl inside a larger bowl full of ice. Have ready a fine-mesh strainer. Combine the milk, sugar, and vanilla seeds in a heavy-bottomed saucepan and bring to a boil. In another bowl, whisk together the egg yolks. At the boil, whisk about ⅓ cup of the milk mixture into the eggs to warm them, then scrape the warm yolks back into the pot of milk. Reduce the heat and cook, stirring constantly, until custard thickens to the consistency of heavy cream. Never stop stirring, always scraping the bottom and sides of the pan with each pass. As soon as the custard has thickened to your liking, strain it into the chilled bowl. Stir periodically until cooled, then refrigerate.

2. To make the meringue: Bring a medium pot of water to a boil. In a large heatproof mixing bowl or the bowl of a stand mixer, combine egg whites, sugar, and salt. Whisk together, then place over the steaming water. Turn off the heat and slowly stir until the whites are warmed and sugar has dissolved (check by dipping a clean finger in). Remove the bowl from pan of water, then whip vigorously (by hand or on high speed of the mixer) until stiff peaks form.

3. Return the water to a simmer. Drop large spoonfuls of the meringue into the water. Poach for 1 to 2 minutes on each side. Don't crowd them in the pan. Remove poached meringues with a slotted spoon, dab the bottoms on a paper towel to remove excess water, and set aside at room temperature. The recipe up to this point can be made a day ahead, and the meringues and cream can be stored separately in the refrigerator.

4. Make the caramel at the last minute. In a small saucepan, mix together sugar and water to a wet-sand consistency. Wipe any stray sugar crystals off the inside of the pan. Place over high heat. Do not stir at all. When it comes to a boil, add the lemon juice, but do not stir (the bubbles will mix it in). Cook until the color changes to a dark amber or caramel color. Turn off the heat.

5. Fill the bottoms of serving bowls with crème anglaise, then float the meringues on top. Using a large spoon, drizzle caramel over the meringue just before serving.

Elsa's Raspberry Snow Queens

Serves 10-12

The 1844 Hans Christian Andersen story of "The Snow Queen" is a classic tale of good versus evil. It is told in seven very long stories about two friends, Gerda and Kai. They grow up as neighbors and friends, but when Kai gets splinters of a magic mirror in his eye, it causes him to see only the bad and ugly. He turns against Gerda and is captured by the Snow Queen. The story follows Gerda's search for Kai, in which she eventually makes her way to Lapland with the help of a reindeer. There she finds Kai frozen solid in a lake. Gerda kisses him, and his tears dislodge the splinter of mirror. As he cries, he defrosts, and slowly remembers his dear friend. You can see why it was so hard to update. This recipe is much easier to interpret than the story was. Deceptively delicious, it is like a sophisticated ice cream with a heavenly crunch and is much more impressive than it is difficult.

2 tablespoons sugar
Grated zest of 1 lemon
1 tablespoon finely minced candied ginger
2 tablespoons framboise liqueur or brandy
2 pints raspberries, divided
2 cups meringue cookies
2 cups heavy cream
Grated dark chocolate for garnish

1. Coat an 8-inch springform pan with nonstick spray, then line with a large sheet of plastic wrap that overhangs the sides. In a food processor or coffee mill, combine sugar and lemon zest. Pulse until the sugar turns yellow.

2. In a small bowl, stir together lemon sugar, candied ginger, framboise, and 1 pint of the raspberries. Stir to dissolve the sugar and break up the berries. Set aside. Break meringue cookies into small chunks and set aside.

3. Whip cream to stiff peaks in a large bowl or stand mixer. Gently fold in raspberry mixture halfway, then add meringue chunks. Continue folding until evenly incorporated. Transfer to the prepared pan and smooth the top. Fold the plastic up and over the mixture. Cover the top with another sheet of plastic. Place in the freezer for at least 8 hours to set.

4. To unmold, warm slightly with your hands before unlocking the springform. Invert onto a serving plate and remove the plastic. Slice into wedges. Serve with remaining pint of whole berries and grated chocolate.

VARIATIONS
Fruit: Use any type of ripe, fresh fruit available. If you're using tropical fruits, consider replacing framboise with dark rum.
Nutty: Replace the berries, framboise, and meringue with chopped almonds, amaretto liqueur, and crushed amaretti cookies. Or try a Nutella swirl, Frangelico liqueur, and chopped hazelnuts.
Mocha: Replace the berries, framboise, and meringue with cocoa nibs and Kahlúa liqueur. Add a tablespoon of espresso powder to the cream.
Cookie: Your favorite cookie is an easy substitute for the meringue.

The Little Mermaid

Le Poisson (Cioppino)

Serves 4-6

"The Little Mermaid" is an 1837 Hans Christian Andersen story revived by Disney in the 1980s. In the original, a mermaid visits the surface of the ocean, where she falls in love with a prince. When his ship sinks, she rescues him, but he's revived by another woman and never learns of the mermaid. Heartbroken, she learns that human lives are shorter than those of mermaids, but while mermaids dissolve into sea-foam at death, humans have eternal souls. Longing for the prince and a soul, she visits a sea witch who provides a potion in exchange for her voice, which gives her human feet. But if the prince does not love her, she would dissolve into sea-foam. Despite a warning that she may never return to the sea, she accepts the potion. Though she befriends the prince, he falls in love with the other woman, and the mermaid's heart is broken. Her sisters offer the little mermaid a magical knife. If she kills the prince and drips his blood on her feet, she'll be a mermaid again. She can't do it, and becomes sea-foam. Disney avoided the overt Christian themes, and rather than present a tragedy, gave us a happy ending. This recipe is a celebration of the song "Les Poissons," which is every chef's favorite Disney song.

2 tablespoons olive oil
1 yellow onion, diced
1 fennel bulb, diced
3 cloves garlic, minced
3 bay leaves
1 teaspoon fennel seed, toasted
and ground
2 tablespoons chopped fresh
oregano
1 sprig fresh thyme
1 teaspoon crushed red pepper
flakes
1 teaspoon sea salt
½ teaspoon cracked black pepper
One 28-ounce can crushed peeled
tomatoes
1½ cups dry white wine
1 cup clam juice or fish stock
1 cup water
1 pound white fish
(cod, haddock, tilapia), cubed
1 pound large shrimp, peeled
and deveined
1 pound mussels or clams
(or a combination) scrubbed,
desanded, and debearded
1 pound calamari bodies,
cut into rings
¼ cup chopped Italian parsley

1. Heat oil in a large heavy skillet over high heat. Add onion and fennel. Sauté until translucent, about 10 minutes. Add garlic, bay leaves, fennel seed, oregano, thyme, red pepper flakes, salt, and pepper and cook until onions are soft. Add tomatoes, wine, clam juice, and water. Cover. Bring to a boil. At the boil, reduce heat to low and cook for 10 minutes.

2. Add fish, shellfish, and calamari. Cover and cook for 3 to 5 minutes, until shrimp are pink and mussel or clamshells open. Remove from heat. Remove bay leaves and thyme sprig. Stir in parsley.

Ursula's Tentacle Salad

Serves 4-6

The Little Mermaid is a movie credited with resuscitating Walt Disney Studios. Its success is due to the use of Walt Disney's original formula for success—pairing well-known stories with relatable themes set to great music. The team of Howard Ashman and Alan Menken, recently off their success in Broadway's *Little Shop of Horrors*, created showstopping Broadway-style song sequences, which became the standard formula in all the films of the Disney Renaissance (1989 to 1999).

The Little Mermaid was the last Disney film to use hand-painted animation cels and the multiplane camera. The film boasted so many hand-painted bubbles (over a million) that the work was farmed out to a Chinese firm, the offices of which were adjacent to Tiananmen Square. While the world watched China's student uprising unfold on television in 1989, Disney wondered if the bubbles would survive. This episode is partially responsible for the company's complete switch to Pixar's Computer Animation Production System (CAPS) in all subsequent films.

Disney reimagined Andersen's sea witch as a half-human, half-octopus creature named Ursula, an amalgamation of both the mythological creature Cecaelia (half human, half octopus or squid) and the drag performer Divine (of John Waters film fame).

1½-2 pounds squid (calamari) rings and tentacles
2 tablespoons olive oil
Grated zest and juice of 1 lemon
2 cloves garlic, minced
½ cup sour cream
2 tablespoons dried dill
½ teaspoon sea salt
½ teaspoon cracked black pepper
½ red onion, diced
4 green onions, chopped
3 Persian cucumbers, diced
2 stalks celery, diced
1 cup cherry tomatoes, halved
½ red bell pepper, diced

1. Bring a medium saucepan of water to a boil over high heat. Add calamari and cook for 2 to 3 minutes, until opaque but still tender. Drain and submerge calamari in ice water to prevent overcooking. Set aside.

2. In a large bowl, mix together oil, lemon zest and juice, garlic, sour cream, dill, salt, and pepper. Add chopped vegetables. Toss to coat. Drain calamari, pat dry, and add to vegetables. Toss to coat. Season to taste. Serve chilled.

Empire Biscuits

Makes 6-8

Brave, about a Scottish princess navigating life and family responsibility, achieved many firsts for Disney. Produced at Pixar, it was that studio's first fairy tale, the first to feature dialogue in Gaelic and Scots, their first female protagonist, the first teenager, and the first without a romantic interest. It's also the first Pixar film to put a woman, Brenda Chapman, in the director's chair of a feature film, leading to the first woman to win the Academy Award for Best Animated Feature. The story is about a headstrong girl, the firstborn of the medieval Scottish clan DunBroch. Her father encourages her in the tomboyish things she loves, including archery. But her mother considers her behavior unbefitting a princess. It's a theme that resonates with parents of teenage daughters—encouraging strength and autonomy in girls, while at the same time being frustrated by it. Unhappy with her parents' plan to marry her off, Mérida runs into the woods and comes across the Will-o'-the-Wisp, an apparition that misleads travelers. It leads her to a witch, who gives her a magic cake that turns her mother, Queen Elinor, into a bear. The spell can only be reversed if Merida can "mend the bond torn by pride." It is a sweet tale that is especially touching to parents of teenage daughters.

The following recipe is an obsession with Merida's little brothers, Hamish, Hubert, and Harris. In real life, they're Scotland's interpretation of a linzer cookie—two shortbreads sandwiched with jam, covered in icing, and topped with a cherry. Because they originated in German-speaking central Europe, they were originally known as German or Deutsch biscuits. But because Germany was the enemy in World War I, the name was changed to the more patriotic "empire."

1½ cups all-purpose flour
¾ cup powdered sugar
10 tablespoons (1¼ sticks, 5 ounces) unsalted butter
2 tablespoons milk
1 tablespoon kirschwasser brandy
1 tablespoon lemon juice
Pinch sea salt
8 ounces powdered sugar, sifted
6 to 8 tablespoons raspberry jam
3 or 4 candied cherries, cut in half

1. To make the cookies: Preheat oven to 400°F. Line a baking sheet with parchment paper. In a large bowl, mix flour and powdered sugar. Add butter, cutting it in with a fork, or your clean fingers, for a crumbly mixture. Continue kneading until a dough just forms.

2. Turn dough out onto a floured surface. Knead briefly into a flat disk. Roll out to a thickness of about ⅛ inch. Using an offset spatula, loosen the dough from the work surface. Cut out 2- or 3-inch circles with a biscuit cutter and place them on the prepared baking sheet. Bake for 10 to 15 minutes, until the edges are just golden. Cool.

3. To make the icing: Whisk together milk, kirschwasser, lemon juice, salt, and powdered sugar. Mix to a thin but spreadable consistency, adjusting as necessary with more sugar or more water. When cookies are cool, pair them up. To fill and decorate the cookies: Spread icing across the top of one of each pair of cookies. Spread a tablespoon of raspberry jam on the other. Sandwich together and top with a piece of candied cherry in the center.

Merida's Sticky Toffee Pudding

Serves 10-12

Another first for *Brave* was new software created by Pixar to illustrate Merida's hair. It allowed the hairs to bounce and interact with the environment in an incredibly realistic way. The studio also created three original tartans, one of which was entered into Scotland's official tartan registry. (This was not Disney's first registered tartan—Clan McDuck got one in 1942.)

This dessert is claimed by many regions of Britain, including Scotland, where the most famous version can be found at the Udny Arms Hotel in Newburgh, Aberdeenshire. The hotel, a historically significant landmark, is named for Clan Udny of the seventeenth century, who held a castle and barony in the region. This pudding, which is cake-like in texture, is a historically significant dessert, made sweet and rich by the addition of dates, an ingredient made available through imperial colonization.

CAKE

1½ cups dates, chopped
1¼ cups boiling water
1½ cups all-purpose flour
1 teaspoon baking powder
½ teaspoon baking soda
½ teaspoon sea salt
4 tablespoons unsalted butter
1 cup sugar
1 teaspoon vanilla extract
2 eggs

TOFFEE SAUCE

1 cup sugar
½ cup corn syrup
1 tablespoon unsalted butter
2½ cups heavy cream

Vanilla ice cream for serving

1. Preheat oven to 350°F. Coat a 9 x 13-inch baking pan with spray. Combine dates and boiling water in a bowl. Set aside to plump for 10 minutes.

2. Combine flour, baking powder, baking soda, and salt. Set aside.

3. Cream together butter and sugar until smooth and lump free. Add vanilla, then eggs, beating after each addition. Add dry ingredients and softened dates, alternating in three increments. Transfer batter to prepared pan and bake for 20 minutes, until firm. Let cool, turn out onto a rack, then cut into squares.

4. To make the toffee sauce: Combine sugar, corn syrup, and butter in a large saucepan. Set over high heat and bring to a boil, without stirring, until the mixture turns a dark amber or caramel color. Off heat, stir in cream and mix until smooth.

5. To serve, douse squares of cake with toffee sauce and top with a scoop of vanilla ice cream if you prefer.

Dragon Fruit Pops

Makes about 18

The animated film, *Mulan*, is based on an ancient Chinese poem, "The Ballad of Mulan." It tells of a female warrior who replaces her father during compulsory enlistment for military service. The poem is thought to have originated during the Northern Wei dynasty, 386 to 534 CE. It was first transcribed during the sixth century, dramatized as a play during the Ming dynasty in the sixteenth century and written as a historical novel during the Qing dynasty of the seventeenth century.

In the original poem, Mulan, trained in martial arts, swordsmanship, and archery, leaves for battle with her parents' blessing, In some interpretations, Mulan fights for twelve years and is not detected as a female. In others, she's promoted to general after ten years, and then reveals her womanhood before a battle, instantly garnering respect from her soldiers who are inspired to win the battle. Other versions are darker, revealing the death of her father upon her return, and with his loss, her heart is broken. Another tells of the distress caused by her memories of battle and her subsequent suicide. Worst of all, one recounts her capture and service as a concubine to the Huns, also resulting in suicide.

The stories are important to China, providing inspiration to real soldiers and periodically revived when the country needs motivation. Mulan's popularity is evidenced in many movies, plays, novels, and monuments (she even has a crater on the planet Venus). Disney's version, however, is not a favorite in China, as many feel it strays too far from the original.

Released in 1998, *Mulan* was the first film entirely produced at Walt Disney Feature Animation Florida, which up until then had mainly worked on shorts. The animators took a research trip to China to record its culture, architecture, landscape, landmarks, and people, to make the film look authentic. The result was an animation style harkening back to classic Chinese watercolor and ink painting. They also used the latest technology, which enabled animators to easily create amazing crowd effects. The initial Disney story focused on Mulan's dissatisfaction with her place in Chinese society and her enlistment as an attempt to avoid an arranged marriage. But believing the character was not sympathetic enough, they reverted to the more traditional telling of Mulan, with her ultimate goal to protect her family and country.

1 ripe red or white dragon fruit
1 cup plain yogurt
1 cup coconut milk
2 tablespoons honey

1. Cut dragon fruit in half and scoop the flesh into a blender. Add yogurt, coconut milk, and honey. Puree until very smooth. Transfer to Popsicle molds, insert sticks, and freeze for at least 4 hours, or until firm enough to unmold.

Mulan

Mushu's Smiling Breakfast

Serves 4

Mulan is the only Disney princess who is not born of, nor married to, royalty. Therefore, she is not actually a princess. It is the only Disney film to use the phrase "cross-dresser," and the only one to feature warfare. Although there was no dragon sidekick in the original story, Mushu was conceived as comic relief in the tradition of Robin Williams as the genie in the film *Aladdin*. Initially, the dragon was larger than a horse, but concealing such a creature from the other soldiers would be next to impossible. So the animators made Mushu pocket-size. Voiced by Eddie Murphy, Mushu was the actor's first voice work. He went on to voice Donkey in the DreamWorks Animation film *Shrek*, released in 2001.

Congee is a classic Asian comfort food and a staple in many countries. In China, it's known by different names, depending on the region, including *zhān* and *báizhōu*, meaning white porridge. It's made with rice that has been cooked until very soft and broken down. The toppings vary by region too, and whether it is being eaten as comfort food or for medicinal therapy (used much like chicken soup is in the West), it's still "happy to see you."

2 cups water

1 tablespoon freshly grated ginger

1 clove garlic, minced

½ teaspoon sea salt

¼ teaspoon cracked black pepper

1½ cups cooked long-grain rice

4 eggs

4 strips bacon, cooked

¼ cup chopped shallot

½ cup roughly chopped fresh cilantro

Soy sauce for serving

1. In a large saucepan, combine water, ginger, garlic, salt and pepper. Bring to a boil. Add cooked rice. Reduce heat and simmer for 20 to 30 minutes, until the rice is very soft and thick. Remove from heat. Cover to keep warm.

2. Bring a second pot of water to boil. Cook the eggs for 7 minutes for soft-boiled, or to desired doneness. Transfer to a bowl of ice water and chill. When they are cool enough to handle, peel and half. Rewarm bacon if necessary.

3. Divide congee between four bowls. Top each with two halves of soft-boiled egg and a bacon strip. Serve with shallots, cilantro, and soy sauce on the side for your guests to add as they like.

The Gray Stuff (Pâté de Campagne)

Serves 10-12

"Beauty and the Beast" has ancient origins, with some linguists placing it in the pre-Germanic Bronze Age. It has been interpreted many times in plays, operas, film, television, and literature, but was first written down by Gabrielle-Suzanne Barbot de Villeneuve, in 1740. This first version, written to entertain the French nobility, involved fairies, animal servants, and enchanted rooms with lavish trappings. But the theme was sibling rivalry and greed, unlike Disney's version, which is a warning against judging a book by its cover. And in the original, the beast was rejected, not because he was ugly or scary but because he was stupid.

The tale most familiar to us comes from a retelling of Villeneuve's story by Jeanne-Marie Leprince de Beaumont in 1757. It was geared toward children, focusing primarily on preparing young girls for arranged marriages. The Disney version, released in 1991, combines this later version with a famous 1946 live-action film by Jean Cocteau.

Disney's *Beauty and the Beast* was its first feature to use three-dimensional computer-generated backgrounds with traditionally animated characters. For audiences at the time, the ballroom scene was breathtaking. They placed traditionally rendered characters into a three-dimensional environment, an incredibly magical effect. This effort was rewarded with *Beauty and the Beast* being the first Disney film to win the Golden Globe Award for Best Motion Picture. It also won two Academy Awards for its music (title track and score), and it was their first Academy Award nomination for Best Picture since *Mary Poppins*.

This is a classical French interpretation of country-style pâté. "Try the gray stuff, it's delicious!" Rough in texture, like an American-style meatloaf, pâté de campagne is meant to be served in small pieces atop a slice of baguette, with a dollop of Dijon mustard and a cornichon pickle or two.

2 tablespoons unsalted butter
½ cup diced pancetta
1 cup minced white onion
2 cloves garlic, minced
2 teaspoons fresh thyme leaves, roughly chopped
1½ teaspoons freshly grated nutmeg
10-12 slices bacon
2½ pounds ground pork
2 eggs
⅓ cup heavy cream
2 teaspoons sea salt
1 teaspoon cracked black pepper
¼ cup cognac or good brandy
2 cups diced ham
Dijon mustard for serving
Cornichon pickles for serving
Sliced baguettes for serving

1. Melt butter in a heavy skillet over medium heat. Add pancetta. Cook until fat is rendered and meat begins to brown. Add onion, garlic, thyme, and nutmeg. Cook until onion is translucent. Remove from heat and set aside to cool.

2. Line a 9 x 5 x 3-inch loaf pan or ceramic terrine with bacon slices. Lay slices in the bottom, across the short width, starting in the center, so that the slices overlap the edge of the pan, to be wrapped around the filling. Set aside.

3. Combine ground pork and eggs in a large bowl. Mix thoroughly. Add cream, salt, pepper, cognac, and cooled pancetta mixture. Mix very well.

4. Place one-third of pork mixture in the bottom of bacon-lined pan. Press gently. Layer half the ham evenly across the surface. Add another one-third of pork mixture, spread evenly, and top with remaining ham. Finish with remaining pork. Spread evenly, tapping gently to remove any air bubbles. Fold bacon strips up over the top.

5. Preheat oven to 350°F. Cover pan tightly with foil. Set into larger 13 x 9 x 2-inch baking pan. Carefully add 2 inches of water to the bottom pan. Place in oven and bake 2 hours, until internal temperature reaches 155°F. Cool, then refrigerate, preferably overnight. For a firm, dense texture, weight the top of the pâté with a heavy skillet and a few cans of food. The next day, slice pâté. Serve with Dijon mustard, cornichon pickles, and sliced baguette.

Mrs. Potts's Tea-Poached Salmon

Serves 4

Enchanted household items were not a part of the original tale but were added by Disney to bring light-hearted comedy into a story that is traditionally very dark. Angela Lansbury, who voiced the character of Mrs. Potts, worked on this film between episodes of her television series, *Murder, She Wrote*. When asked to sing the song "Beauty and the Beast," she did not believe she was the right choice for such a tender ballad. Nevertheless, she agreed to record one version as a backup, which ended up in the film. This recipe is an homage to the beloved teapot, and her voice, which, according to Lansbury, is still recognized as that of Mrs. Potts by children all over the world. "Off to the cupboard with you now, Chip."

¼ cup (or 4 bags) green tea
4 cups boiling water
1 tablespoon vegetable oil
1 tablespoon sesame oil
Four 6-ounce salmon fillets
2 cloves garlic
One 1-inch piece ginger, grated
1 pint enoki mushrooms
8 ounces Japanese long beans, cut into 3-inch lengths, or green beans
Grated zest and juice of 1 lemon
2 tablespoons ponzu sauce
4 green onions, chopped
Sea salt to taste

1. Combine tea bags and boiling water in a teapot. Remove from heat and set aside to steep for 10 minutes. (The tea should be stronger than you would normally drink it.) Remove tea bags and set aside at room temperature.

2. Heat oils in a heavy-bottomed skillet over medium heat. Add salmon fillets, skin-side down, and cook until crisp, about 2 to 3 minutes. Flip fillets over. Add the garlic, ginger, and enough tea to come halfway up salmon fillets. Bring liquid to a boil, reduce to a simmer, and cover the skillet tightly. Poach over low heat for 10 minutes, or to desired doneness.

3. Remove salmon from pan. Cover to keep warm. Increase heat and reduce liquid to a tablespoon or two. Add enoki mushrooms and sauté for 4 to 5 minutes, until golden. Add beans. Continue to sauté 2 to 3 minutes, until the beans are bright green and tender. Remove from heat. Add lemon zest and juice, ponzu sauce, onions, and salt. Serve salmon, skin-side up (the skin is edible and delicious), preferably on a bed of sautéed vegetables.

10

Movie Magic

Nothing brings magic to life like the silver screen. Our own imaginations are all well and good, but film allows us to view the imaginations and inventiveness of others, helping to expand our own imaginations. Today, special effects are such that, when depicting magical elements coming to life, we can almost believe that magic is real. But special effects have been used since the beginning of film. Techniques such as stop-action substitution, split-screen masking, and double exposure have been convincing moviegoers that magic is real since the 1890s. Personally, I find the older films much more enjoyable. Sure, the effects are obviously fake. And yes, that is a wire you see suspending the flying witch in a harness. But this just speaks to the magic of the storytelling and the skill of the makers. Somehow, we can still find enjoyment, hope, love, and inspiration in these old-timey films. The following recipes feature the most endearing representations of magical, mystical film, old and new.

Chocolate Pancakes

Serves 2-3

Witches have been historically portrayed as a threat to normalcy, as outcasts or predators, feared for centuries. Some films continue to perpetuate that history, but *Practical Magic* uses it to offer hope. Not a big hit when released in 1998, it developed a following because it celebrates women. A black comedy based on the book by Alice Hoffman, it has a stellar cast—Sandra Bullock, Nicole Kidman, Stockard Channing, and Dianne Wiest. The plot centers around sisters Sally and Gillian Owens, their eccentric aunts, and a witch's curse. In colonial Massachusetts, a pregnant witch is run out of town, exiled to an island. Abandoned by her lover, she casts a spell to prevent falling in love again. But the spell is a curse to future generations of Owens women—any man who falls in love with them dies.

Fast-forward to today. The sisters live in a town fearful of their family and history. They navigate life, love, heartbreak, and the bonds of sisterhood, questioning whether the lasting love of a man is necessary (witchcraft here is a metaphor for independent women who defy societal expectations). In the end, we conclude, more than anything else, that women need other women. Bad stuff happens when the women don't have each other. It's only when the women of the town come together that the town, and the family, is saved. Sadness comes not from lack of romance, but from lack of belonging.

The Owens women don't care about convention. They eat what they want, when they want. And their Aunt Frances's declaration, "In this house we have chocolate cake for breakfast. We never bother with silly things like bedtimes and brushing our teeth," is every kid's dream come true. Since most parents are not freethinking witches, you can compromise with these chocolate pancakes.

1¼ cups all-purpose flour
¼ cup cocoa powder, preferably extra dark
1 teaspoon sea salt
¼ cup sugar
2 teaspoons baking powder
3 large eggs, separated
1 teaspoon vanilla extract
3 tablespoons coconut oil, melted butter, or vegetable oil
1½ cups milk
2 cups maple syrup
1 cup chocolate chips
Butter for serving

1. In a large bowl, sift together flour, cocoa powder, salt, sugar, and baking powder. In a separate bowl, whisk together egg yolks, vanilla, oil, and milk. In a third large bowl, whisk or beat egg whites to stiff peaks.

2. Add the wet ingredients (except for the egg whites) to the dry. Stir with a few vigorous turns of the whisk (do not overmix—lumps are just fine). Add one-third of the egg whites and mix briefly. Fold in remaining egg whites. Again, it's okay if there are lumps and streaks of egg whites. Let the batter sit at room temperature for 10 minutes while you preheat a griddle on medium-high heat.

3. Heat maple syrup in a small saucepan over medium heat until simmering. Remove from the heat and stir in chocolate chips until melted, then set aside.

4. Test griddle by cooking a tablespoon of batter. The pancake should take a full minute to produce bubbles on the surface before it's flipped. If it puffs and browns too quickly, reduce the heat. If too slowly, increase the heat. Cook for another minute once flipped, until it feels firm to the touch. Judging brownness is tricky with chocolate batter, so rely on touch and aroma. When the heat's right, cook ¼ to ⅓ cup of the batter for each pancake. Serve with warm chocolate-maple syrup and butter (or whipped cream and a cherry—because there are no rules!).

Hocus Pocus

Clark Bars

Makes about 2 dozen

Imagine a comedy about three witches who eat children! That's the premise of the 1993 Halloween classic, *Hocus Pocus*. Campy, fun, and a bit horrifying, its underlying theme is the importance of family. In colonial Salem, just before three witches are hanged for the crime of eating children, they manage to cast a spell. If a virgin lights a certain candle under a full moon, they will come back to life. Obviously, this happens centuries later, on Halloween night, when Max, who is forced to take his annoying little sister, Dani, trick-or-treating, tries to impress a girl. The Sanderson sisters are summoned. But in order to be permanently resurrected, they have to suck the life out of a child before sunrise.

Trying to murder children doesn't sound funny, but the witches, Winifred, Sarah, and Mary (played by Bette Midler, Sarah Jessica Parker, and Kathy Najimy, respectively), are befuddled by the modern world. They are impeded at every turn by things like sprinklers, vacuum cleaners, asphalt, and daylight saving time. Comedy aside, the recurring theme in the film is about the complicated relationships of siblings. The events begin with siblings in colonial Salem, and the theme is echoed in the modern era. Even the witch sisters are, despite their squabbles, loyal to each other. Typical Disney.

Garry Marshall plays a neighbor in a devil costume and is mistaken by the sisters for the real Satan. Hilarity ensues. He hands out full-size Clark Bars to trick-or-treaters, which Mary mistakes for chocolate-covered fingers of a man named Clark. Here's a homemade version of the candy bar, which was the first combination bar, with a central core surrounded by chocolate. Its popularity skyrocketed when sent to American troops in World War I and World War II, when it was considered essential to the war effort.

2 cups peanut butter
4 cups graham cracker crumbs
1 cup melted butter
1 cup chopped peanuts
½ teaspoon sea salt
1 tablespoon lemon juice
2 cups powdered sugar, sifted
One 14-ounce can sweetened condensed milk
2 cups chocolate chips

1. Coat a 8 x 12-inch brownie pan with nonstick spray. In a bowl, cream together peanut butter and graham cracker crumbs until well mixed. Add melted butter, peanuts, salt, lemon juice, and powdered sugar. Mix thoroughly to form dough. Press into prepared pan.

2. Combine sweetened condensed milk and chocolate chips in a small saucepan. Melt over medium heat, stirring continuously until thoroughly mixed. Pour on top of the peanut butter mixture and spread evenly. Chill for 1 to 3 hours, until very firm. Cut into 1 x 3-inch bars and serve.

Emerald Lobster Rice Salad

Serves 4

This 1939 film, based on the bestselling book *The Wonderful Wizard of Oz* by L. Frank Baum, was made partly because Metro-Goldwyn-Mayer Studios wanted to compete with the blockbuster 1937 Disney film *Snow White and the Seven Dwarfs*. Critical response to *The Wizard of Oz* was favorable, and "Over the Rainbow" won the Academy Award for Best Original Song. But it lost Best Picture to *Gone with the Wind*, falling far behind the Civil War drama in ticket sales. Because of its extravagantly high production costs, *The Wizard of Oz* was not profitable. Not until it began showing annually on television, in 1959, did it become the classic we think of today.

This film about magical creatures and a quest to find the wizard was altered from the original book in several significant ways. Most iconically, the color of Dorothy Gale's slippers changed from silver to red to better demonstrate the new Technicolor process. And many of the scarier elements were left out for fear of frightening children, including wolves, bees, and a giant spider. In the book, the Emerald City is green, because the wizard makes everyone wear green-tinted glasses. The dressing for this salad is based on the classic green goddess.

2 cups water

1 cup long-grain jasmine rice

2 cups chopped Italian parsley leaves, divided

1 teaspoon sea salt, divided

1 pound asparagus or broccoli (or ½ pound of each)

½ cup mayonnaise

½ cup buttermilk

1 cup chervil leaves

½ cup tarragon leaves

½ cup chopped chives

2 scallions

3 anchovy fillets

Grated zest and juice of 1 lemon

¼-½ cup olive oil

2 cups cooked lobster, langostino, or shrimp meat

1 cup shelled edamame or fresh green peas

1. Bring the water to a rolling boil in a large saucepan. Add rice, 1 cup of the parsley, and ½ teaspoon of the salt. Reduce heat to low. Cover tightly. Cook for 20 minutes, until rice is tender and has absorbed the water. Remove from the heat, transfer to a large bowl, and cool completely.

2. Bring another pan of water to a boil. Add a pinch of salt and asparagus. Cook until bright green and just tender, about 5 minutes. Drain and shock in a bowl of ice water. When cold, drain from ice water and cut into pieces.

3. Combine mayonnaise, buttermilk, remaining parsley, chervil, tarragon, chives, scallions, anchovies, lemon zest and juice and ½ teaspoon salt in a blender. Pulverize until smooth adding enough oil for a dressing consistency.

4. Toss dressing with cooled rice and mix well. Add lobster, edamame, and asparagus. Adjust seasoning. Serve chilled with a wedge of lemon if you prefer.

VARIATIONS

Grains: Rice is nice, but there are so many interesting grains that can be substituted, including quinoa, millet, or kamut.

Veggie: Omit the seafood. Replace it with cooked and drained beans of your choice.

Bell, Book and Candle

Greenwich Village Pizza Pyewacket

Makes 2 pizzas

This 1958 comedy is based on a play written by John Van Druten. Gillian Holroyd (played by Kim Novak) is a single, nontraditional woman and a modern witch. Her independent streak is manifested in her beatnik wardrobe and her intelligence (she has a degree in anthropology and runs a shop full of African and Oceanic art). In this universe, a witch who falls in love would lose her powers. However, depressed and restless, Gillian uses her cat (a traditional witch's familiar), Pyewacket, to cast a spell that makes her neighbor, Shep Henderson (played by James Stewart), fall madly in love with her.

Witchcraft is equated with the counterculture, set in the bohemian mecca of Greenwich Village. Typical of the 1950s, the story ends with real love and conformity to traditional roles. Gillian loses her powers, and with it, her unique qualities. Even her wardrobe changes, shifting from the barefoot-beatnik look to a feminine dress. The ending provides love, but erases her individuality. Just a few years later, the film would inspire the television show *Bewitched*, in which the character of Samantha happily retains her agency.

Some of the best scenes in the film take place in the Zodiac Club, a groovy underground haven for witches, warlocks, and all those who don't conform. Greenwich Village still has an air of nonconformity, as well as some of the best pizza in town.

DOUGH

1⅓ cups warm water
1 envelope (2½ teaspoons)
active dry yeast
2 teaspoons honey or sugar
2 tablespoons olive oil
1 teaspoon sea salt
3 - 4 cups bread flour

SAUCE

¼ cup olive oil
2 cloves garlic, minced
1 tablespoon dried oregano
1 tablespoon dried thyme
½ cup fresh basil leaves
1 teaspoon sea salt
½ teaspoon cracked black pepper
One 28-ounce can
whole peeled tomatoes

TOPPINGS

Fresh mozzarella, sliced
Fresh basil leaves, snipped
Extra olive oil to finish

1. To make the dough: In a large bowl, mix together water, yeast, and honey. Set aside until bubbly, about 10 minutes. Stir in oil, salt, and 1 cup of flour, and mix into a paste. Continue adding flour until you create a soft dough that pulls away from the side of the bowl. Turn out onto a floured surface. Knead 8 to 10 minutes, until smooth and elastic. Cover with a warm, damp towel. Set aside, at room temperature, until doubled in volume, about an hour. Divide dough in half, knead each half into a ball, set them on a floured surface, and cover to rise for another hour. (Up to this point, the recipe can be done a day ahead, and the dough can be left to rise a second time slowly in the refrigerator.)

2. To make the sauce: Heat oil in a large skillet over high heat. Add garlic, oregano, thyme and basil. Cook until fragrant but not browned, 30 seconds to 1 minute. Add salt, pepper and tomatoes. Stir, crushing the tomatoes, until mixture comes to a boil. Reduce to a simmer and cook, stirring occasionally, until the sauce thickens, about 10 minutes. Remove from the heat and cool.

3. Preheat oven to 475°F. Coat two pizza pans or baking sheets with nonstick spray. Place risen dough on a floured surface and roll out as far as you can with a rolling pin. Rest it briefly, and then continue to roll, or stretch, until about 12 inches in diameter. Repeat. Place dough on prepared pans. Slightly crimp edges. Spread sauce across surfaces in a thin layer. Distribute mozzarella evenly across the top, sprinkle with basil and a drizzle of olive oil. Bake for 10 minutes, or until the dough is golden brown and the cheese is melted and bubbling.

182

Three Little Pigs in a Blanket

Makes about 1 dozen

Historically, fairy tales reinforce societal expectations, morality, and gender roles. The wicked are ugly and are punished. The good are beautiful and live happily ever after. The film *Shrek*, however, champions the power of accepting yourself for who you are, and embracing your perceived shortcomings. This DreamWorks Animation film is loosely based on a 1990 fairy tale picture book written by William Steig. An ogre, Shrek, finds his swamp overrun by fairy tale creatures that have been banished by the corrupt Lord Farquaad. Determined to save their home, as well as his own, Shrek cuts a deal with Farquaad to get the princess Fiona to be his bride. With the help of Donkey, he sets out to rescue Princess Fiona, who is not what she appears to be. The pleasure of this film lies in its unrelenting parodies of other fairy tales and tropes. References to other films and television—and the occasional break through the fourth wall—give this ostensibly children's film an adult edginess that resonates with crowds, as evidenced by three sequels, two holiday films, a stage play, and a spin-off film, *Puss in Boots*.

The three little pigs appear throughout the Shrek franchise, pigging out, partying, and under a blanket. Somehow, their thick German accents make them even funnier. In honor of the pigs' Bavarian heritage, enjoy this recipe for pretzel dogs.

2 quarts water
1 pound French bread dough or pizza dough, homemade or store-bought
One 14-ounce package mini sausages (such as Hillshire Farm Lit'l Smokies) or small slices of sausage
¼ cup baking soda
1 tablespoon sugar
4 tablespoons melted butter
2-3 tablespoons best medium-coarse sea salt
Mustard or cheese sauce to garnish

1. Preheat oven to 400°F. Coat a baking sheet with nonstick spray. Bring water to boil in a large saucepan.

2. Meanwhile, roll out dough to ¼-inch thick and cut into strips about ½ x 2½ inches. Coil the strips around the sausages, leaving the ends visible. Use a little water to glue the dough in place.

3. At the boil, turn water down to a simmer. Add baking soda and sugar. Drop the dough-wrapped sausages into the water and poach for about 15 seconds. Remove with a slotted spoon, tap off excess liquid, and place on the baking sheet. Repeat with remaining wrapped sausages (do not crowd them in the poaching liquid).

4. Brush poached sausage wraps with melted butter, sprinkle with salt, and bake for 10 minutes. Rotate the pan so they brown evenly and finish baking for another 10 to 15 minutes, until golden brown. Serve with mustard.

Matilda

Trunchbull Chocolate Cake

Serves 8-10

Matilda Wormwood is a genius. At six years old, though mistreated by her family, she finds solace in books. When she's allowed to go to school, she finds herself in the hands of tyrannical principle, Miss Trunchbull, at Crunchem Hall, whose motto is, "When you are having fun, you are not learning." Author Roald Dahl confronts the vulnerability and powerlessness of childhood in his book *Matilda*, on which the film is based. She stands up to her oppressors with the help of telekinesis and a teacher named Miss Honey. The evil in the book was too ridiculous to be believed, but the film reimagining of it is also at times upsetting. Billed as a dark family comedy, it underscores the oppression Matilda faces and is a success story for underdogs everywhere.

Principal Trunchbull is violent, locking students in solitary confinement, and spinning them by their pigtails. When an overweight boy, Bruce Bogtrotter, sneaks a piece of chocolate cake, he's punished by being forced to eat an entire cake. In the film, it's one of the chocolatiest cakes imaginable. While the punishment is cruel, one can't help but wish for a taste. With added coffee to heighten the bitterness of dark chocolate, and a light, delicate crumb, this cake is a reward, not a punishment.

CAKE

1 cup unsalted butter, softened
1¾ cups granulated sugar
2 large eggs
2 cups all-purpose flour
¼ cup cocoa powder (extra dark if possible)
1 teaspoon baking soda
½ teaspoon sea salt
1½ cups buttermilk
1 teaspoon vanilla extract

FROSTING

½ cup unsalted butter
2/3 cup cocoa powder
(extra dark if possible)
1 teaspoon vanilla extract
3 cups powdered sugar, well sifted
1/3 cup whole milk

SYRUP

1 cup strong brewed coffee
1 cup granulated sugar

1. Preheat oven to 350°F. Line two 8-inch round cake pans with nonstick spray, cut circles of parchment paper to fit the bottoms, insert into the pans, then spray the paper.

2. In a large bowl, cream together butter and granulated sugar until smooth and lump free. Add eggs, one at a time, mixing well between each addition.

3. Sift together flour, cocoa powder, baking soda, and salt. In a measuring cup with a spout, combine the buttermilk and vanilla. Alternate adding dry and wet mixtures to the butter mixture in three increments, stirring well between each addition. Transfer the batter to the prepared pans and smooth the tops. Bake for 30 to 45 minutes, until risen and firm. A toothpick inserted into the center should come out clean. Remove from oven and cool completely. Turn out the cakes.

4. To make the frosting: Melt butter in a small pan on the stove or in the microwave. Transfer to a mixing bowl. Add cocoa powder and vanilla. Blend thoroughly. Alternate adding powdered sugar and milk, beating to a fluffy consistency. (You can add a little more milk or a little more powdered sugar, if necessary, to achieve a good frosting consistency.)

5. To make the syrup: Combine coffee and granulated sugar in a small saucepan. Bring to a boil, then remove from heat and set aside.

6. To assemble, place one cake layer on a serving plate. Drizzle with coffee syrup. Spoon one quarter of the frosting in the center and smooth evenly out to the edges using an offset metal spatula. Place the second cake layer on top. Drizzle again with syrup. Put half the remaining frosting on top, spread it out to the edges, then over the edges and onto the sides. Make a thin, even coat of frosting first (called a crumb coat). Use the rest of the frosting to make decorative, swooping marks for a homemade look. Despite what you see in the movie, I suggest serving slices on a plate with a fork.

Turkish Delight

Makes about 2 dozen

C. S. Lewis was inspired to write *The Lion, the Witch and the Wardrobe* when his family boarded children during World War II. He followed up with six sequels and prequels from 1950 to 1956. Though he didn't believe a film could do his world justice and he never sold the rights, in 2005, Walden Media and Walt Disney Studios acquired them from his estate. In *The Lion, the Witch and the Wardrobe*, the youngest of four Pevensie children, Lucy, discovers a wardrobe, through which she enters the land of Narnia. She encounters Mr. Tumnus, who, rather than turn her over to the evil White Witch, sends her home. Her siblings don't believe her, but brother Edmund follows her into the wardrobe, discovering Narnia himself. He's enticed by the White Witch with tea and Turkish delight to give up his siblings in return for a suggestion that he can become king of Narnia. Turkish delight was a mark of status in late Victorian England. It was difficult to make and imported from the East. During World War II, sugar and candy rationing made such treats exceedingly rare. In Narnia, Turkish delight is a perfect enticement for greedy Edmund Pevensie.

PAN #1

1½ cups water
1 tablespoon lemon juice
4 cups granulated sugar

PAN #2

2 cups water
1 teaspoon cream of tartar
1 cup cornstarch
1 tablespoon rose water
2 drops pink or red food coloring
¼ cup cornstarch
1 cup powdered sugar

1. Coat a 9 x 13-inch brownie pan with nonstick spray. Line it with wax or parchment paper, so that the edges extend out of the pan. Then spray the paper as well.

2. To make the sugar syrup: In a large saucepan, combine water, lemon juice, and granulated sugar. Bring to a boil. Insert a candy thermometer and cook to 240°F (soft-ball stage). Turn off the heat and let stand.

3. In a second pan, combine water, cream of tartar, and cornstarch. Stir to dissolve. Bring to a boil, stirring vigorously (use a handheld mixer if possible, as stirring gets tiring), until the mixture is very thick. Turn off the heat and slowly add the sugar syrup, a little at a time, whisking with each addition, until it is smooth.

4. When sugar mix is in, turn the heat back on. Bring back to a boil, stirring slowly. Reduce to a simmer and cook for about 30 minutes, stirring occasionally, until thick, semitranslucent, and beginning to detach from the pan. Turn off the heat.

5. Off the heat, add rose water and food coloring and mix in thoroughly. Transfer to the prepared brownie pan. Tap to drive out air bubbles and smooth the surface. Set aside to completely cool.

6. In a large bowl, combine cornstarch with powdered sugar. Sift it over the surface of the Turkish delight, and onto the work surface. Turn the pan out onto the dusted surface and coat the bottom (now the top) with the cornstarch mixture. Using an oiled and dusted pizza wheel, cut into 1-inch strips, then into 1-inch cubes. Toss each cube into the sugar/starch mixture to coat. Eat or store in an airtight container fully coated in sugar/starch mixture at room temperature.

VARIATIONS
Use a variety of extracts or floral waters (such as orange flower). You may also add up to 1 cup of chopped nuts at the same stage.

11

Television Spells

In 1941, commercial television was first broadcast in the United States. That must have seemed pretty magical to the seven thousand people nationwide who owned television sets at the time. By 1951, the number rose to twelve million. By 1955, half of American households had televisions. By the 1990s, most Americans had televisions, broadcasting for an average of seven hours per day.

The first popular shows were borrowed from network radio and included variety shows such as *The Jack Benny Program*, Milton Berle's *Texaco Star Theatre*, and children's programming, like *The Howdy Doody Show* and *The Mickey Mouse Club*. By the mid 1950s, situation comedies, game shows and news programs dominated the airwaves. Of these early hits, there were only two shows working in a fantasy genre, *Topper* in 1953, about a stuffy banker living in a haunted house, and *The Twilight Zone* in 1959, an anthology of fantasy, science fiction, and suspense tales. It was not until the 1960s that America was ready to accept magic into their homes on a regular basis.

Uncle Arthur's Napoleon

Makes 10

In 1964, Sol Saks created a classic American sitcom, *Bewitched*, about a young housewife who was also a witch. Elizabeth Montgomery starred as Samantha Stephens, whose family disapproved of her marriage to a mortal. Her husband, Darrin (played by Dick York and Dick Sargent), can barely tolerate her powers, or her relatives. Storylines involved spells gone awry but happily resolved by the end of each episode. *Bewitched* was on the air for eight seasons and set a template for future television sitcoms. The appeal was its ability to relate magic to the problems that young couples had in the 1960s, when the role of women was being questioned. *Bewitched* presented a powerful, independent woman, and a husband who had difficulty dealing with that power—something men of the era were also coping with.

Sam's Uncle Arthur, played by Paul Lynde, is a frequent visitor to the Stephens home, popping up in unlikely places—in an ice bucket, on the stove, or in a pot of stew. He is a practical joker whose powers always cause problems. During a dinner party for Darrin's boss, Uncle Arthur appears in the oven, ruining Samantha's angel food cake. He flubs his spell to create a replacement Napoleon dessert, conjuring the real Napoleon Bonaparte instead. This recipe will cause far less trouble.

One 17-ounce box frozen puff pastry (2 sheets), thawed but cool

PASTRY CREAM

1 egg
2 egg yolks
½ cup granulated sugar
¼ cup cornstarch
1 teaspoon sea salt
2 cups milk
1 vanilla bean, scraped
4 tablespoons unsalted butter

GANACHE

1 cup chopped dark chocolate or chocolate chips
1 cup heavy cream

FILLINGS

1 cup raspberry jam
1 cup sweetened whipped cream (store-bought or homemade)

Powdered sugar for dusting

1. Preheat the oven to 400°F. Line a large baking sheet with parchment paper. Unroll the puff pastry and lay both 10 x 15-inch rectangles onto the prepared pan, at least 1 inch apart. Place another parchment sheet on top, and then lay a second baking sheet directly on top of the parchment. This will ensure that the pastry holds its rectangular shape and rises evenly. Bake for 10 minutes. Check for doneness. Return to the oven if necessary for 5 to 8 more minutes, until well risen and evenly browned. Uncover and cool completely.

2. To make the pastry cream: Combine egg, yolks, granulated sugar, cornstarch, and salt in a bowl. Whisk until smooth. Combine milk and vanilla in a saucepan and bring to a boil. Pour ¼ cup of warm milk mixture into the egg mixture, stir briskly, and then return egg mixture to the saucepan (this is called tempering). Reduce heat to low, and whisk continuously until mixture thickens, 1 to 2 minutes. Remove from heat. Stir in butter, then strain into a bowl. Cover with plastic wrap pressed directly onto the surface (this prevents a skin from forming) and cool completely.

3. To make the ganache: Place chopped chocolate in a heatproof bowl. In a saucepan, bring cream to a boil. Pour over chocolate. Let sit, undisturbed, for 3 minutes, then whisk smooth. Set aside at room temperature.

4. To assemble, slice each puff pastry sheet into thirds (to make six 5 x 10-inch strips). Slice each of those pieces into five smaller rectangles (to make thirty 5 x 2-inch rectangles). Each Napoleon will be made with three rectangles (for a total of ten servings). For each serving, pipe pastry cream on the bottom of a rectangle. Spread another rectangle with jam, and then pipe on whipped cream and place on top of the first rectangle. Spread the top rectangle with ganache and place it on top of the cream layer. Chill. Serve with a dusting of powdered sugar.

Dr. Bombay's Chicken Tikka Masala

Serves 4

One common plot device used to cause confusion in the Stephens home was illness. When strange symptoms of a magical disease appeared (such as striped skin), a call to the witch doctor was in order. "Calling Dr. Bombay! Calling Dr. Bombay! Emergency! Come right away!" was the incantation that brought forth Dr. Hubert Bombay, played by Bernard Fox. In addition to his corny jokes and buxom nurse assistants, Dr. Bombay always showed up in a crazy costume, having been interrupted doing something bizarre while on call. In addition to the many bathrobes and towels from having been summoned from the bath, he arrived in swimsuits from swimming with dolphins and sharks, a jockey outfit from riding ostriches, a Roman toga, a matador costume, formal tuxedos, clown costumes (he was clowning around with his nurse), and numerous football uniforms (from tackling his nurse). The shapely nurses would not go over well in the twenty-first century, but it is a little comforting to know that in a *Tabitha* spin-off, he married one of them.

6 cloves garlic, minced

4 tablespoons freshly grated ginger

2 tablespoons ground turmeric

2 tablespoons garam masala

2 tablespoons ground cumin

1 tablespoon ground coriander

1 tablespoon sea salt

1½ cups plain yogurt

2 pounds boneless, skinless chicken breasts, sliced in lengthwise strips

3 tablespoons ghee or vegetable oil

1 yellow onion, diced

6 cardamom seeds, ground

2 dried red chile peppers, chopped, or ½-1 teaspoon crushed red pepper flakes

One 28-ounce can whole peeled tomatoes

¼ cup tomato paste

2 cups heavy cream

¾ cup fresh cilantro, chopped

1. Combine garlic, ginger, turmeric, garam masala, cumin, coriander, and salt in a small bowl. Toss to mix. Place half of this spice mix in a large zip-top bag and add yogurt and chicken. Seal. Massage to blend, then refrigerate to marinate for at least 4 to 6 hours, or overnight.

2. Heat ghee in a skillet over medium-high. Add onion, remaining spice mix, cardamom, and chile peppers and cook, stirring, until well caramelized. Add tomatoes and tomato paste. Continue cooking over medium heat, stirring and smashing the tomatoes for 10 to 15 minutes. Add cream and cilantro. Continue cooking on low heat until thickened, 20 to 30 minutes.

3. Meanwhile, cook marinated chicken strips in broiler or over a grill, flipping to evenly color, until firm and cooked through. Cool slightly, then slice into bite-size pieces. Add to sauce and cook for 10 minutes. Serve over basmati rice, sprinkled with extra cilantro, and warm naan if preferred.

Cocoa Beach Coconut Shrimp

Serves 4

After the success of *Bewitched*, the other networks scrambled to find a show that could compete. For NBC that show was *I Dream of Jeannie*. From 1965 to 1970, magical shenanigans took an exotic form, with plots that took full advantage of the post-Kennedy space craze. United States Air Force Captain Tony Nelson (later promoted to Major) crashes his one-man capsule near a deserted island in the South Pacific. There he finds a bottle on the beach, rubs it, and releases Jeannie (played by Barbara Eden). Having been trapped inside for two thousand years, she falls in love and vows to serve him. Episodes revolve around Jeannie's desire to please Captain Nelson and his attempts to hide her. As with *Bewitched*, *I Dream of Jeannie* was on when Betty Friedan's *The Feminine Mystique* was a bestseller, challenging the idea that the only fulfillment for American women was the role of wife and mother. A woman calling a man "master" on TV, fulfilling his wishes, and pining for his love did not fit feminist ideals. But Jeannie isn't a slave or a servant. She stays with Captain Nelson because she loves him. In fact, she regularly defies him, doing what she thinks is right, or funny, and he deals with the consequences. The show is set in Cocoa Beach, Florida, south of Kennedy Space Center. Celebrate the Space Age with this classic Florida recipe.

2 pounds large shrimp (26/30 per pound), peeled and deveined
3 cloves garlic, minced
2 tablespoons freshly grated ginger
2 tablespoons Worcestershire sauce
Zest and juice of 1 lemon
1 tablespoon Creole seasoning
One 14-ounce can coconut milk

ORANGE CHILI SAUCE

½ cup orange marmalade
One 8-ounce can crushed pineapple
⅓ cup red chili sauce
½ teaspoon sea salt
½ teaspoon cracked black pepper
Grated zest and juice of 1 lime
15-20 wooden skewers, soaked in water for at least 1 hour
1 cup shredded coconut

½ cup chopped fresh cilantro for garnish

1. To make the shrimp skewers: Combine shrimp, garlic, ginger, Worcestershire, lemon zest and juice, and Creole seasoning in a large zip-top bag. Massage to mix, then add coconut milk. Refrigerate to marinate for 4 to 6 hours, or overnight.

2. To make the orange chili sauce: Combine marmalade, pineapple, chili sauce, salt, pepper, and lime zest and juice in a bowl. Mix thoroughly. Set aside.

3. Preheat grill or broiler on high heat. Thread shrimp onto skewers. Roll each skewer in shredded coconut and place on the grill or a broiler pan. Cook for 3 to 5 minutes, turning halfway, until the shrimp are pink and firm. Sprinkle skewers with chopped cilantro and serve with a side dish of orange chili sauce.

The Jeannie Martini

Serves 2

This cocktail is the perfect blend of mid-century modern and contemporary mixology. Serve it in your best martini or coupe glasses for maximum impact.

2 ounces vodka
2 ounces pink grapefruit juice
2 ounces pomegranate juice
1 ounce lime juice
1 ounce simple syrup
Fresh strawberries for garnish

1. Combine vodka, juices, and simple syrup in a cocktail shaker with ice. Shake vigorously, then strain into coupe or martini glasses. Garnish with strawberries.

Bundt Friday Cake with Truth Sprinkles

Serves 10-12

Based on an Archie Comics spin-off, *Sabrina the Teenage Witch* was a live-action television show that ran from 1996 to 2003. Set in Massachusetts, the half-mortal, half-witch Sabrina Spellman was being raised by her aunts in the Boston suburb of Westbridge. On her sixteenth birthday, she learned of her powers and the true whereabouts of her parents (exiled by the Witches Council for their mixed marriage). Each week, Sabrina, played by actress Melissa Joan Hart, had to balance being a teenager with having powers—powers that, as it turned out, could not solve every teenage problem. For seven seasons, viewers watched her navigate life like every other kid, with added wacky magical hijinks. It was a nice premise, and a reassuring one for kids, who were no doubt relieved to learn that even witches must endure mean girls, homework, and life lessons.

A classic example is the episode from the first season, "Bundt Friday." To ascertain what lies are being spread by mean girls, Sabrina takes advantage of her home economics project and covers the assigned chocolate Bundt cake with "truth sprinkles." Everyone ate it, and, of course, the truth hurt. Feelings were revealed about friends and crushes, and when the cake made its way into the teachers' lounge, true callings were revealed. Ignorance really can be bliss! Silly and eye-rolling (especially when a teacher encouraged students to "smell your neighbors' Bundts"), it was everything we love about magic TV.

CAKE

1 cup cocoa powder (preferably extra dark)
1 cup brewed coffee, warm
3 cups all-purpose flour
1 tablespoon baking powder
1 teaspoon sea salt
1 cup (2 sticks) unsalted butter, at room temperature
2½ cups sugar
4 eggs

GANACHE

1½ cups chopped dark chocolate or chocolate chips
1½ cups heavy cream

Colorful sprinkles for finishing

1. To make the cake: Preheat oven to 350°F. Grease and flour a standard Bundt pan. In a bowl, whisk together cocoa powder and coffee. Set aside to absorb. In a separate bowl, sift flour, baking powder, and salt together. Whisk.

2. In a third bowl, cream butter and sugar until smooth and lump free. Add eggs one by one, mixing thoroughly between each addition. Alternate adding flour mixture, then coffee mixture, to butter mixture in three increments, beating thoroughly between each addition.

3. Transfer batter to prepared pan. Bake for 30 to 45 minutes, until firm and a toothpick inserted comes out clean. Cool for 5 minutes, then invert onto a rack, remove the pan, and cool completely.

4. To make the ganache: Place chocolate in a large, heatproof bowl. In a saucepan, bring heavy cream to a boil. Pour over chocolate. Let sit, undisturbed, for 3 minutes. Whisk smooth. Set aside at room temperature until you're ready to decorate.

5. Place cake on a serving platter and drizzle ganache over the top. Cover with sprinkles and serve. A scoop of vanilla ice cream, if you prefer, will only enhance the magic.

Salem's Black Cat Cocktail

Serves 2

Sabrina lives with her two aunts, Hilda (Caroline Rhea) and Zelda (Beth Broderick), as well as their cat, Salem, a 500-year-old warlock, whose sentence for planning world domination is to live as a cat. Salem is mischievous, but also clearly loyal to Sabrina, helping her study for her Witch's License and offering advice for navigating life. Drink to Salem with this not-so-classic cocktail, perfect for your Friday the 13th party.

2 ounces vodka
1 ounce kirschwasser or other cherry brandy
1 ounce blue curaçao
2 ounces cranberry juice
1 tablespoon lime juice
3 ounces lemon-lime soda
Strips of lime zest for garnish
Blueberries for garnish

1. Combine vodka, kirschwasser, curaçao, cranberry juice, and lime juice in a cocktail shaker with ice. Shake well, and then strain over ice into two tumblers. Top with lemon-lime soda. Garnish with lime zest and blueberries.

Drell's Pot Roast

Serves 4-6

Sabrina's Aunt Hilda is the most colorful character in the series. Ditsy, eccentric, and fun-loving, Hilda is anything but subtle, always producing explosions with her spells. Real-life magician Penn Jillette plays her ex-fiancé, Drell, who is also the head of the Witches Council. They date on and off, despite his frequent cancellations, signaled by the appearance of a pot roast. (He sends half a pot roast when he's running late.) Hilda puts up with this until she finally takes the "Test of True Love," discovers she no longer loves Drell, and ends the relationship for good. This recipe is a much bigger sign of love than Drell ever offered.

2-4 tablespoons olive oil
One 3- to 5-pound chuck roast
1 large yellow onion, sliced into wedges
3 cloves garlic, minced
2-3 sprigs fresh thyme
2-3 sprigs fresh rosemary
3 bay leaves
2 cups red wine
2 cups beef broth
4 large carrots, cut into ½-inch coins
4 red potatoes, quartered
1 teaspoon sea salt or to taste
1 teaspoon cracked black pepper or to taste

1. Preheat oven to 300°F. Heat oil in a large, heavy-bottomed Dutch oven over high heat. Add roast and sear on all sides until browned. Remove meat to a platter. Add onion to the pot and cook, stirring, until translucent, about 10 minutes. Add garlic and herbs, and cook, stirring, until fragrant.

2. Add wine, stirring and scraping the bottom to deglaze. Add beef broth. Bring to a boil. Add beef, reduce to a simmer, cover, and transfer to the oven. Bake for 2 hours. Add carrots and potatoes to pot and cook for another hour, until everything is fork tender. Before serving, season with salt and pepper.

VARIATIONS
Alternate Meats: Use the same recipe with a lamb roast. For pork, use white wine instead of red. For a whole chicken, cut into parts, and reduce cooking time to 2 hours total.
Alternate Liquids: Instead of red wine, try this with beer, cider, coffee, or Coca-Cola. The bitter and sweet liquids are especially good for fatty cuts of meat.

Buffy the Vampire Slayer

Willow's Roasted Marshmallow Bars

Makes about 1 dozen

In 1992, a film written by Joss Whedon called *Buffy the Vampire Slayer* was released. It told the story of a typical high school cheerleader named Buffy Summers, chosen to be next in a long line of vampire slayers. The script was dramatically altered from Whedon's original, removing dialogue thought to be too highbrow, and turning the film into a comedy rather than horror. Whedon walked off the set. Then, in 1997, he created a darker, smarter television series that was true to his original vision. In it, Buffy, played by Sarah Michelle Gellar, just wanted to live a normal life but had to battle the forces of evil. She was endowed with remarkable strength, stamina, accelerated healing, agility, and the ability to return from the dead. On the outside, Buffy appeared to be the type of character that falls victim in every horror film—ditsy, ignorant, and eventually dead. But here she was elevated to a bad-ass hero fighting a monster of the week that was usually a pastiche of classic works of horror, myth, and folklore. All this, and high school angst too.

Buffy was always helped by the Scooby Gang of socially outcast friends. As the seasons progressed, we were introduced to many demon enemies, other slayers, vampires both good and bad (including her love interest, Angel, the vampire with a soul and a spin-off). Willow Rosenberg, played by Alyson Hannigan, began as a shy, absent-minded nerd. But eventually it became clear she had magical abilities, and she began to study witchcraft, going through many changes including being seduced by dark forces in the sixth season. She was also one of the first popular television characters to be portrayed as a lesbian. Like the rest of the Scooby Gang, Willow constantly referenced food. In one episode, when it was suggested that they set fire to a group of bad boys-turned-demons, Willow giddily produced the marshmallows. Celebrate this show's perfect blend of comedy and action with these luscious marshmallow bars.

1 cup (2 sticks, 8 ounces)
unsalted butter
1 cup brown sugar
1 cup granulated sugar
3 large eggs
1 tablespoon vanilla extract
2 teaspoons baking soda
1 teaspoon sea salt
2 ⅔ cups all-purpose flour
1 cup chocolate chips
15-20 large marshmallows

1. Preheat oven to 350°F. Coat a 9 x 13-inch brownie pan with nonstick spray.

2. In a stand mixer, or in a large bowl with a hand mixer, beat butter and sugars until smooth and lump free. Add eggs, one by one, mixing thoroughly after each addition. Stir in vanilla, baking soda, salt, and flour. Fold in chocolate chips.

3. Place half the batter in the pan and spread evenly. Place marshmallows across the top, with 1 inch of space in between, then fill in the gaps with dollops of the remaining batter.

4. Bake for 20 to 30 minutes, until marshmallows are roasted and batter is firm. Cool. Slice into squares.

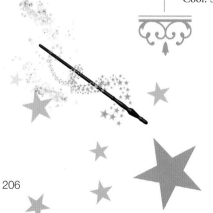

Giles's Jaffa Cakes

Makes 10-12

Buffy was trained by the "watcher" Rupert Giles, a professor of demonology. He researched demons and guided her training. The character (and actor) is English, a source of humor amongst the American teens, especially with regards to food. They ate a lot on the show, and most of the food was easily recognizable to American teenagers. Except for Giles's Jaffa cakes. A British snack cake filled with orange jelly, it is either loved or hated by those that grew up with them. In the case of Giles, it's all love, as evidenced by his delight and distraction when he came across them. The elements of the Jaffa cake are simple: sponge cake, orange jelly and chocolate ganache. Rather than form them into a cookie, this recipe takes a slightly more refined approach, adding orange liqueur and assembling them into individual layered desserts.

JELLY

One 6-ounce box orange-flavored gelatin
1 cup boiling water
½ cup orange juice
½ cup Grand Marnier
Grated zest of 1 orange

GANACHE

1½ cups chopped dark chocolate or chocolate chips
1½ cups heavy cream

SYRUP

½ cup Grand Marnier
½ cup water
1 cup granulated sugar

CAKE

1 cup all-purpose flour
1½ teaspoons baking powder
½ teaspoon sea salt
1 cup (2 sticks, 8 ounces) unsalted butter, softened
Grated zest of 1 orange
1 cup powdered sugar
2 large eggs
1 teaspoon orange flower water
½ cup milk

1. To make the jelly: Line a flat baking sheet or tray with plastic wrap, making sure it comes up and over all sides. In a medium heatproof bowl, combine gelatin and boiling water. Stir to dissolve, then add orange juice, Grand Marnier and orange zest. Mix thoroughly, pour into lined tray, place carefully in refrigerator, and chill completely (at least an hour) until very firm.

2. To make the ganache: Place chopped chocolate in a heatproof bowl. In a saucepan, bring heavy cream to a boil, then pour over chocolate. Let sit undisturbed for 3 minutes. Whisk smooth. Set aside at room temperature.

3. To make the syrup: Combine Grand Marnier, water, and granulated sugar in a small saucepan. Bring to a boil. Set aside to cool.

4. To make cake: Preheat oven to 400°F. Line baking sheet with parchment paper. Coat ten to twelve 3-inch pastry rings (or muffin tins) with nonstick spray. Set on prepared baking sheet. Sift together flour, baking powder, and salt. Set aside.

5. In a stand mixer, beat butter, orange zest, and powdered sugar 3 to 5 minutes until light and fluffy. Add eggs, one at a time, mixing thoroughly between each addition. Add orange flower water. Add flour mixture, alternating with milk in three increments, mixing thoroughly after each.

6. Transfer batter to prepared rings. Bake for 10 to 15 minutes, until golden brown and a toothpick inserted comes out clean. Cool slightly, remove rings while still warm, and cool completely.

7. To assemble, use a pastry ring to cut circles from the set jelly. Slice cakes in half, horizontally. Brush syrup on the bottom layer, place a jelly circle on top, followed by the second cake layer. Brush again with syrup. Finish with a dollop of ganache. Smooth ganache and make a crosshatch design with a fork. Chill before serving.

Spike's Buffalo Wings

Serves 2-4

The character of Spike, played by James Marsters, is a bad guy/good guy, goofball, love interest, and vampire. Dressed in leather, with slick, bleach-blond hair, he's a demonic version of Billy Idol (who, Spike explains, stole his look). Despite tending toward violence more than other vampires, he's unusually passionate, starting out life as an aspiring poet. These complexities are manifested in his history of killing slayers and his on-again, off-again romance with Buffy. One quirky character trait is his love of normal human food, including the frequent platter of spicy chicken wings. This recipe will put a little demonic punk swagger in your step.

2 pounds chicken wings
2 tablespoons olive oil
1 tablespoon paprika
1 teaspoon garlic powder
1 teaspoon sea salt
1 teaspoon black pepper
1 teaspoon dried thyme
¼ cup hot sauce
2 tablespoons honey
2 teaspoons unsalted butter
Blue cheese or ranch dressing
Celery sticks

1. In a large zip-top bag, combine wings with oil, paprika, garlic powder, salt, pepper, and thyme. Massage the bag to distribute the flavors, then refrigerate to marinate for 4 to 6 hours, or overnight.

2. Preheat oven to 400°F. Line a baking sheet with a rack, and then set wings on top, evenly spaced. Roast until crispy, 50 to 60 minutes. Halfway through roasting, turn wings for even browning.

3. Meanwhile, combine hot sauce, honey, and butter in a small saucepan. Heat, stirring, until butter is melted. Transfer sauce to a large bowl. When the wings are ready, add them to the bowl and toss to coat. Return wings to the oven. Broil for 3 minutes, to caramelize the sauce. Serve hot with a dipping bowl of dressing and celery sticks.

12

Alchemists and Magicians

An ancient form of scientific experimentation, alchemy played a significant role in the development of modern chemistry. Early civilizations believed four elements—earth, water, air, and fire—were present in all life forms, and if they could be manipulated, the nature of life could be controlled to treat illness and make precious metals. In other words, get rich and live forever. By manipulating ingredients in search of such transmutations—for example, by heating them—alchemists produced new things like alcohol, alloys, pigments, perfumes, cleaning products, dyes, and more. Alchemy also gave birth to astrology, astronomy, and therapeutics—but silver, gold, and eternal life remained elusive.

An eighth-century Arabic alchemist, Jabir ibn Hayyan (also known as Geber), theorized that transmutation could occur with the help of a substance known as the philosopher's stone. He got the idea from the mythical Emerald Tablet carved by Hermes Trismegistus (Hermes the Thrice-Greatest, associated with the Greek god Hermes and the Egyptian god Thoth), said to have contained the secrets of the universe, including instructions for creating the philosopher's stone. In Jewish, Christian, and Islamic traditions, Seth, son of Adam, received the instructions from God from a tablet clutched in the hands of Trismegistus's corpse. Jabir ibn Hayyan claimed to have translated it into Arabic under the title *The Second Book of the Elements of the Foundation*, translated into Latin in the twelfth century. It eventually got into the hands of European alchemists, such as Sir Isaac Newton, who continued the search for immortality and bling.

Geber

Silver White Cake

Serves 8-10

One reason alchemists believed in transmutation stems from the fact that we can witness such natural changes—ice turns to water, food becomes part of us, base metals can be extracted from ore when smelted, as well as change form and color with heat. The hope was that if such changes could be controlled, they might be able to turn common, inexpensive base metals into precious silver and gold. But without the philosopher's stone, these transmutations were not possible.

Silver white cake was synonymous for white cake in the mid-twentieth century. The cake is white because it is made with egg whites, not yolks. The recipe is a sister to yellow cake, made with only egg yolks. When cake mixes became popular, *silver* and *gold* were the words used to market the products. Today, they are sold as white and yellow cake in most markets. A recipe for silver white cake appeared as early as 1871 in *Mrs. Porter's New Southern Cookery Book*. In the 1950s, it appeared in several cookbooks, including the *Betty Crocker Cookbook*, as well as magazines, such as *Good Housekeeping*.

CAKE

1¼ cups milk
½ teaspoon almond extract
½ teaspoon vanilla extract
5 egg whites
2¼ cups cake flour
1⅔ cups sugar
1 tablespoon baking powder
1 teaspoon sea salt
¾ cup (1½ sticks, 12 ounces) unsalted butter or shortening, at room temperature

BUTTERCREAM

1 cup egg whites
1½ cups sugar
Pinch sea salt
2¼ cups (4½ sticks, 18 ounces) unsalted butter, softened
½ teaspoon vanilla extract

Silver sprinkles for finishing

1. To make the cake: Preheat oven to 350°F. Coat two 8-inch round cake pans with nonstick spray, line the bottom of each with a circle of parchment paper, and spray the paper too.

2. Combine milk, almond extract, vanilla, and egg whites in a bowl. Mix to combine thoroughly. Set aside.

3. Combine flour, sugar, baking powder, and salt in the bowl of a stand mixer (or use a handheld mixer). Mix to combine. Add butter, mixing in slowly. Add milk mixture slowly, in two or three increments, beating for 3 to 5 minutes.

4. Divide batter equally between prepared pans. Bake for 20 to 30 minutes, until a toothpick inserted comes out clean. Cool slightly and remove from pans. Cool completely.

5. To make the buttercream: Bring a medium pot of water to a boil. In the bowl of a stand mixer, or using a handheld mixer, combine egg whites, sugar, and salt. Whisk briefly. Place over the steaming water. Turn off heat. Gently stir until whites are warmed and sugar is dissolved (check by dipping a clean finger in). Remove from pan of water. Whip vigorously on high speed until mixture is cool and stiff peaks form. Slowly but steadily, while whipping, add chunks of softened butter until incorporated. Whip for 2 to 3 minutes longer, until mixture has a smooth, fluffy, frosting texture. Slowly mix in vanilla. Keep at room temperature until ready to use.

6. Place one cake layer on a serving plate. Spoon one quarter of buttercream in center. Smooth evenly to edges with an offset metal spatula. Place second cake layer on top. Put half remaining frosting on top, spread it to edges, then over edges and onto sides. Give a thin, even coat of frosting first (called a crumb coat) then use the rest of the frosting to smooth and fill. Finish with sprinkles.

Geber

Legal Golden Honey Loaf

Serves 10-12

The alchemist's hope was to harness a prime material—used to create everything in the universe—in order to possess the power of transmutation. This process could then transform death to life, banish illness, turn quartz to diamond, and turn iron to gold. But governments began to worry that if artificial gold could be easily produced, it would debase the value of currencies. King Henry IV of England outlawed alchemy in 1404, but it continued underground, and alchemical writing became deeply coded. By the time of Sir Isaac Newton's death, it was maligned. Chemists began distancing themselves from the focus of gold making, which was by then disreputable. The result was a rebranding of alchemy from science to pseudoscience. This recipe for golden honey loaf cake contains no actual gold and will not get you arrested. It will, however, make you very popular.

½ cup golden raisins
½ cup dried currants
¼ cup rum
3 cups all-purpose flour
2 teaspoons baking soda
1 teaspoon sea salt
1 cup (2 sticks, 8 ounces) unsalted butter, softened
1 cup sugar, plus more for sprinkling
¾ cup honey, divided
1 teaspoon ground cardamom
1 teaspoon ground nutmeg
¼ teaspoon ground cinnamon
¼ teaspoon ground clove
4 large eggs
1 cup milk
½ cup sliced almonds
1 tablespoon hot water

1. Preheat oven to 350°F. Coat a 9 x 13-inch cake pan with nonstick spray. Line it with parchment paper (just the bottom of the pan is fine). Spray the paper.

2. Combine raisins, currants, and rum in a small bowl. Set aside to plump. Sift together flour, baking soda, and salt in another bowl. Set aside.

3. Combine butter and sugar in the bowl of a stand mixer (or use a handheld mixer). Beat until smooth and lump free. Add ½ cup of the honey, cardamom, nutmeg, cinnamon, and clove. Beat until well mixed. Add eggs, one at a time, mixing thoroughly after each addition. Add flour mixture, alternating with milk in three increments, mixing thoroughly after each addition. Fold in plumped raisins last.

4. Transfer batter to prepared pan. Top with sliced almonds and a sprinkle of granulated sugar. Bake for 30 to 45 minutes, until golden brown and firm. A toothpick inserted should come out clean.

5. Combine remaining ¼ cup honey with hot water. Stir to liquefy. Brush over the hot cake, evenly and slowly, until all is absorbed. Cool completely before slicing.

Nicolas Flamel

Elixirs of Life

Quantities vary by container

Known as Dumbledore's friend in the Harry Potter books, Nicolas Flamel was a real person. Many believe he was an alchemist who succeeded in finding the philosopher's stone, the key to transmutation. Active in Paris in the fourteenth and fifteenth centuries, he was a scribe and bookseller known for his philanthropy. Not until centuries after his death did rumors start circulating about his success as an alchemist.

The legend of Flamel describes a book of hieroglyphics he couldn't decipher. He went to Spain in search of a translator, and the book was identified as *The Book of Abramelin*, written by an Egyptian mage (magic maker). It contained the formula for the philosopher's stone. With it, Flamel and his wife were able to create silver and gold. The rumored "proof" was that his philanthropy was only made possible by that wealth. Believers claimed to have sighted him after his death, reinforcing the idea that he had created the elixir of life and was immortal. In the seventeenth and eighteenth centuries, Flamel became a legendary figure within both alchemical and literary circles.

In many respects, modern chemistry has created elixirs of life with medicine. Early attempts to prolong life were made with tinctures—concentrated liquid herbal or spice extracts used medicinally—that can have real-life benefits today. But they're most interesting when used as flavoring agents. They are a great addition to your pantry or bar cart and make great gifts.

Assorted herbs and spices, such as:
Chamomile: assists digestion, relaxation
Cinnamon: antioxidant, anti-inflammatory
Citrus zest: aids digestion, immune system
Fennel seeds: assists digestion, cramps, nausea
Ginger: relieves nausea, heartburn
Lavender: antioxidant, aids relaxation
Peppermint: aids digestion, gas, headaches
Rose petals: soothes sore throat, antioxidant
Sage: aids sore throat, anti-inflammatory
Turmeric: relieves inflammation
Vanilla: aids digestion, alleged aphrodisiac

80-proof vodka, light rum, or apple cider vinegar
Honey as desired

1. Fill small glass bottles or jars half full of one herb or spice. Add a small amount of boiling water, just to moisten, which helps release beneficial oils. Fill with alcohol to the rim of the container, cap and give it a shake.

2. Store in the refrigerator for at least 6 weeks, shaking daily to extract flavors and beneficial oils. When the tincture is ready, add a teaspoon of it to sparkling water, ginger ale, or tea. Sweeten with a teaspoon of honey. Or use as an extract to flavor your favorite baking or cocktail recipes.

Sir Isaac Newton

Lemon Mercury Torte

Serves 6-8

We remember Sir Isaac Newton as the founder of modern science, a revolutionary who created calculus, quantified gravitational attraction, described the laws of motion, and revolutionized optics by proving that white light is a mix of spectral colors. Less known is that for decades he secretly investigated alchemical theories, which was forbidden under English law.

Many reasons are given for Newton's secret experiments on the transmutation of metals, but the most reasonable is simply that he was a scientist. The seventeenth century was all about man using technology to understand nature. Alchemy was really just a theory of matter, figuring out the components of substances, and understanding what the Earth and the universe are made of. Not so weird. But by changing material particles around, man was changing nature, which was God's territory. Similar to modern feelings about bioengineering, alchemists were accused of playing God. So Newton kept his work on the down-low.

Mercury, or quicksilver, is one of the seven metals of alchemy, along with gold, silver, copper, lead, iron, and tin. Alchemists witnessed mercury's dramatic reaction in nitric acid, creating a red vapor over the surface and bright red crystals on the bottom. Because mercury took both solid and liquid forms, they believed that it transcended Heaven and Earth, life and death. It is the only metallic element that takes a liquid form under standard conditions. But it is highly toxic, and many historic figures are now thought to have died from mercury poisoning, including Sir Isaac Newton. Known today mainly from its use in thermometers and barometers, mercury is toxic, prompting most clinical environments to phase out these instruments. This cake has a tart lemon filling that oozes out like mercury, but the only adverse effect will be to your waistline.

LEMON CURD

⅓ cup granulated sugar
⅓ cup lemon juice
Grated zest of 1 lemon
2 large eggs
¼ cup unsalted butter

CAKE

1 tablespoon finely grated lemon zest
½ teaspoon sea salt
1 cup plus 2 tablespoons granulated sugar, divided
1 cup plus 2 tablespoons all-purpose flour
½ teaspoon baking powder
3 eggs

Powdered sugar for dusting

1. To make the lemon curd: Combine granulated sugar, lemon juice, lemon zest, eggs, and butter in a small saucepan. Place over medium heat. Cook, stirring, for about 5 minutes, until the mixture thickens to a pudding consistency. Pass through a strainer into a bowl, then cover with plastic wrap pressed directly on the surface (this prevents a skin from forming). Refrigerate to cool completely.

2. To make the cake: Preheat oven to 350°F. Butter and flour a 9-inch springform pan.

3. Combine zest with salt and 2 tablespoons granulated sugar on a cutting board. Mince very fine until sugar turns yellow. Set aside. Sift together flour and baking powder. Set aside.

4. Combine eggs and remaining 1 cup granulated sugar in the bowl of a stand mixer. Whip together until light and fluffy, 2 to 3 minutes. Add the lemon sugar and whip 1 minute longer. Fold sifted flour mixture into the egg mixture in three increments. Do not overmix.

5. Transfer half the batter to the prepared pan. Spread to cover the bottom. Layer the lemon curd on top, leaving a ¾-inch margin to the edge. Top with remaining cake batter, being sure to enclose all the curd. Bake for 30 to 40 minutes, until golden brown. Cool slightly before unclasping and removing the side of the springform pan. Cool completely before transferring to a serving platter. Dust with powdered sugar.

Diana's Tree

Rock Candy

Makes 5-10, depending on the size of cups used

Alchemists believed that classical Greco-Roman mythology was encoded alchemy. The search for Vulcan's net, an alloy of copper and iron whose crystal structure makes a network pattern on its surface in mythical alchemy, is one example of the quest to decode mythology. Vulcan, the god of fire, discovers his wife Venus in bed with her lover, the god Mars. Vulcan crafts a fine metal net to hang them from the ceiling, so all can witness their shame. This triggered the search for a substance thin as a net but strong as metal, leading to the discovery of Diana's Tree, a special transmutation with a treelike structure of metallic crystals.

To make Diana's Tree, alchemists combined silver with nitric acid, mercury, and distilled water, then let it stand for a month. Slowly, branches rose out, resembling a tree. Sometimes, it produced a fruitlike form on the branches, convincing them that metals were related to organic manner. Diana's Tree was believed to be a precursor to the philosopher's stone and a necessary ingredient for creating it.

There's a substance we use in the kitchen that has properties as magical as Diana's Tree. Sugar goes through a number of transmutations and can be manipulated into many different forms. The following is a sampling of the wonder sugar can do. Use these sugar-coated sticks to sweeten your coffee or tea or to keep your little ones quiet.

1 cup water
3¼ cups granulated sugar, divided
Food coloring (optional)
Candy-flavoring oils or extracts (optional)
5-10 wooden sticks (Popsicle sticks, skewers, or coffee stirrers)
5-10 paper or plastic cups (4-6-ounce size, with openings no larger than 3 inches)
5-10 spring-style wooden clothespins

1. Bring water to a boil in a medium saucepan. At the boil, turn heat down to a simmer. Add 1 cup of the sugar. Stir gently. When it dissolves, add a second cup of sugar. Stir until it dissolves. Repeat with a final cup of sugar. When the sugar dissolves and there are no signs of sugar grains, turn off the heat. Let the mixture stand undisturbed for 15 minutes.

2. If you want to use color and flavor, put a tiny drop in each cup. Moisten one half of each wood stick with water. Dip in remaining sugar to coat with crystals. This is what the candy will grow on. Insert the sugar end into a cup, suspended in the center by inserting the non-sugar end into the second clothespin notch (between the first notch and the spring) and setting the clothespin across the top of the cup. Try to keep the stick off the bottom of the cup.

3. Pour 1 to 2 inches of sugar syrup into each cup. Let stand, undisturbed, for 5 to 7 days, and up to 2 weeks. Crystals will grow slowly up the stick wherever there is granulated sugar. When you have reached the desired crystal growth, dislodge the crystals, and loosen the cup by squeezing the sides gently. Store each stick wrapped in plastic at room temperature.

VARIATION
Instead of using sticks, make the candy on a string. Tie a 5-inch piece of string around the center of a skewer or pencil, dip half in water, and coat with sugar. Place the string in the cup, resting the skewer across the rim. Continue as directed.

Diana's Tree

Honeycomb Candy

Makes about 8 ounces

This candy makes a great garnish for desserts, sprinkled over ice cream or used to decorate cakes. Also known as sponge toffee, it's an easy candy to make, requiring no candy thermometer, fancy molds, or professional techniques. But beware! It acts more like an alchemist's experiment than any other candy method.

1 teaspoon baking soda
½ cup granulated sugar
2 tablespoons corn syrup
1 tablespoon honey
2 tablespoons water

1. Spread a sheet of parchment paper on your counter. Coat with nonstick spray. (Alternatively, if you have a silicone mat, lay it out on the counter.) Sift the baking soda and have it at the ready.

2. In a medium saucepan, combine sugar, corn syrup, honey, and water. Place over high heat. Cook to a golden amber color, about 3 minutes. If sugar browns unevenly, carefully swirl the pot to mix (temperature should be around 300°F, but precision isn't necessary as long as it's golden but not burnt).

3. Turn off heat. Add the baking soda. Stir briefly but vigorously until the sugar erupts like lava, which will happen fast. Immediately, pour the candy onto the prepared counter. Don't spread it—just let it sit, ooze into a blob, and cool. When completely cool, break it into pieces. Store in an airtight container at room temperature or freeze.

Spun Sugar

Makes enough to decorate one large cake or 6-8 small desserts

The pastry chef's most elegant garnish is spun sugar—thin threads of sugar, thicker than hair or cotton candy that can be spun into multiple threads, gathered, and then wrapped around a dessert or bundled into a nest. The process is not hard, but it may take a couple tries to get comfortable working with molten sugar.

1 cup granulated sugar
¼ cup water
2-3 drops lemon juice

1. Line floor with newspaper. Have a rolling pin and fork ready.

2. Combine sugar and water in a small saucepan. Stir to wet-sand consistency. Wipe crystals from inside pan. Place over high heat. Don't stir. At the boil, add lemon juice. Don't stir—it can cause crystallization. When sugar begins to turn golden amber, turn off heat. Let cool for 2 minutes. Dip fork in gently; sugar should flow back into the pot in a steady stream. If it's still drippy, cool a little longer.

3. When sugar is the right consistency, dip in fork. Working over covered floor, whip sugar back and forth quickly over the rolling pin. It should drape down like long strands of hair. Repeat until you have enough to gather with your hands. Form into nests or wrap around a dessert. Repeat. If caramel gets too hard, rewarm gently over low heat. You may develop crystals eventually, but hopefully you've made what you need by then. Clean the pot by filling with water and bringing it to a boil.

VARIATION
To add color, don't cook to amber. Add drops of food coloring as desired while sugar is boiling, at around 290°F. Stop cooking at hard-crack stage (300°F). Proceed as above.

Diana's Tree

Dragon's Beard Candy

Makes about 1 dozen

This hand-pulled cotton candy, originally from China, is made similarly to Chinese hand-pulled noodles. Called *pashmak* in Persian and *kkultare* in Korean, it is a transformation of hard sugar into thin, hairlike threads resembling a dragon's beard. It's fun and not very difficult, as long as the sugar is cooked properly. It may take a couple of tries, but once you get it, you'll be hooked!

1 cup shelled pistachios
2 tablespoons honey
Pinch sea salt
2 cups granulated sugar
¼ cup light corn syrup
½ teaspoon white vinegar
1 cup water
3-4 cups cornstarch
or rice flour

1. Combine pistachios, honey, and salt in a food processor. Grind very fine. Mixture should hold together when squeezed. Transfer to a bowl and set aside.

2. Combine sugar, corn syrup, vinegar, and water in a large, heavy saucepan. Mix into wet-sand consistency. Wipe down inside of pan, so it's clean and free of sugar crystals. Place over high heat. Bring to a boil. Don't stir. If sugar crystals appear on the sides of the pan, brush them away with a clean, wet pastry brush. Cook to 269°F, about 20 to 25 minutes. Turn off heat. Let sugar continue to cook with residual heat to 270°F (on the cusp of hard ball stage).

3. Next, turn the liquid sugar into hard, hockey-puck-shaped blocks. Cool sugar by dipping the bottom of the pan in cool water (not ice). Pour into clean, heat-resistant silicone doughnut molds (about 2 to 3 inches in diameter) or plastic pint containers (with similar footprint). Sugar pucks should be 1 to 1½ inches thick. Cool for about 2 hours at room temperature.

4. Fill a large bowl or tray with cornstarch. Remove sugar blocks from the molds. Dip a puck in cornstarch to evenly coat. Working with fingers (or a tool such as a chopstick), make a hole in the center (if using a doughnut mold, omit this step). If sugar is too firm, microwave 10 seconds at a time until it becomes malleable. Slowly stretch it into a doughnut, dipping it in cornstarch as needed. Slowly and steadily, stretch and turn until the doughnut is about 4 times the diameter of the starting puck (8 to 12 inches).

5. As soon as you can, form a figure eight, then fold it in half, so you have 2 rings. Dip and stretch again, form another figure eight, fold again to get 4 rings. Repeat a total of 11 to 14 times. This will give you thousands of strands. If threads start to break apart, stop and form the candy. The more you practice, the more strands you can achieve.

6. Lay the candy floss on a flat surface dusted with cornstarch. Using scissors, cut into 4-inch sections. Spoon a teaspoon of pistachio mix into center of each section and roll floss around the filling, into a cylinder. Place on serving dish or in paper muffin cups. Store in an airtight container at room temperature.

Harry Houdini

Crystal Ball Cocktail

Serves 1

Harry Houdini is perhaps the best-known magician in history, though he's better described as an illusionist or escape artist. He began performing card tricks at New York's Coney Island, but soon turned to escape acts, finding fame in vaudeville as the Handcuff King. When his act was copied, he moved on to ropes, chains, straitjackets, and other contraptions. His most famous trick was the Chinese Water Torture Cell, in which he was suspended upside down in a locked tank of water.

Houdini never claimed supernatural powers. In the 1920s, he debunked those who did. Paranormal activity was the rage. Many claimed to communicate with the dead via séance, palmistry, divination, and crystal balls. He offered $10,000 to anyone proving such abilities, which was never collected. He hired an investigation team to attend paranormal readings, proving more than one thousand mystics to be cons.

You can create your own crystal balls with spherical ice molds. But as any mixologist will tell you, the key is making it clear. Simply freezing boiled or distilled water won't work because cloudy ice is caused by excess air in the water. Ice freezes from the coldest place first, which becomes perfectly clear. As it freezes, it expands, pushing the air down. In an ice cube tray, the top will be clear and the bottom will be cloudy. The method here creates an exit for excess air, keeping the sphere clear. The cocktail to go with your ice crystal ball is a classic Manhattan.

ICE SPHERE

Individual silicone ice ball mold(s)
Soup or saucepot with handles
that will fit in your freezer
Water (distilled or filtered tastes better
but is not necessary for the effect)
1 wire, long enough to stretch from
one handle of the pot to the other, plus
another 5 inches

1. Fill both the ice ball and the pot with water.

2. Make a simple horizontal loop in the center of the wire, large enough for the ice ball to sit on. Attach wire to both handles of the pot with the loop dipping just below the water's surface.

3. Dunk ice mold into pot, with hole facing down. Pull mold out of water. Set into wire loop, with hole slightly submerged (water will stay inside the ball). Freeze solid. With hole facing down, as mold freezes and ice expands, air-filled water is pushed into the pot.

4. When frozen, remove from mold. Once you have a frozen ball, remove the ridges created by mold. Using a potholder or an oven mitt, heat a butter knife over a flame, such as a gas burner. Use it to smooth lumps and ridges. Return ice to freezer until ready to mix cocktails.

MANHATTAN

2 ounces whiskey
1 ounce sweet vermouth
1-2 dashes Angostura
or orange bitters
1 strip orange zest
1 maraschino cherry

1. Combine whiskey, vermouth, and bitters in a cocktail shaker with ice. Shake vigorously, then strain into a glass over ice sphere. Garnish with orange zest and cherry.

13

Colonial American Magic

American belief in magic was initially a holdover from Europe. Witchcraft, sorcery, and folklore from the old countries existed, but settlers soon developed legends of their own, with a unique American flare. It makes sense, as the settlers found themselves in a strange new land, with new obstacles and new dangers that didn't fit into the stories of their homeland. These tales found their way into the imagination of our earliest authors, who inscribed these legends onto the American psyche.

Washington Irving

Ichabod Crane's Olykoek (Oil Cookies, aka Donuts!)

Makes about 1 dozen

Washington Irving was born in New York City in 1783. His career started with social commentary in local papers, then articles satirizing politics and culture in which we see the name "Gotham" given to the city (an Anglo-Saxon term meaning "Goat's Town" referencing foolish residents). One of his pseudonyms, Diedrich Knickerbocker, has since been used in reference to New Yorkers (and their basketball team). Irving achieved fame for a collection of stories titled *The Sketch Book of Geoffrey Crayon, Gent.*, in which "Rip Van Winkle" and "The Legend of Sleepy Hollow" appeared. It's also here we read of St. Nicholas flying over a town in a wagon, later fleshed out by others into Santa Claus. Irving wrote more compilations, as well as *A History of the Life and Voyages of Christopher Columbus*, a mix of fact and fiction popularizing the idea that Columbus's contemporaries believed in a flat Earth. Irving traveled extensively, completing stories of the Alhambra, the Moors, and the Prophet Muhammad. He served as the U. S. ambassador to Spain and the first chairman of the Astor Library, which became the New York Public Library. The last thing he wrote was a five-volume biography of his namesake, George Washington. He inspired many other authors, including Longfellow, Poe, Hawthorne, and Melville.

In "The Legend of Sleepy Hollow," Ichabod Crane is smitten with the richest girl in town, Katrina Van Tassel. She seems to have warm feelings for him, so he proposes at a harvest festival but is turned down. Feeling her attentions were faked to make Brom Van Brunt jealous, Ichabod left for home alone, downhearted. On the way, he encountered the Headless Horseman, who threw his own head and knocked Ichabod off his horse. In the morning, all that was found was his hat, his horse and a shattered pumpkin. Ichabod is portrayed as a poor, lanky, superstitious schoolteacher. His penchant for old Dutch wives' tales is matched only by his appreciation for their food, as it was the custom for townspeople to care for schoolteachers. In Sleepy Hollow, settled by the Dutch in the early seventeenth century, he would have been served olykoeks, a traditional Dutch fried dough, similar to a donut (but without the hole).

1 cup mixed dried fruit
½ cup rum
Warm water as needed, plus 2 tablespoons
1 cup whole milk
1½ packages active dry yeast
Pinch plus ½ cup granulated sugar, divided
1 egg
1 egg yolk
4 tablespoons unsalted butter
1 teaspoon freshly ground nutmeg
1 teaspoon sea salt
5 cups bread flour, divided
3-4 cups vegetable oil
Powdered sugar for dusting

1. In a small bowl, combine fruit, rum, and enough warm water to cover fruit. Set aside for at least 30 minutes (but longer is better, and overnight is best).

2. In a large bowl, mix milk, yeast, 2 tablespoons water, and a pinch of sugar. Set aside until bubbly, about 10 minutes. Stir in egg and yolk, remaining ½ cup granulated sugar, butter, nutmeg, salt, and 1 cup flour. Mix into a paste. Drain and add plumped fruit, then continue adding remaining flour until you create a soft dough that pulls away from the side of the bowl. Turn onto a floured surface. Knead for 8 to 10 minutes, until smooth and elastic. Cover with a warm, damp towel and set aside at room temperature until double in volume, about 1 hour.

3. When the dough has doubled, turn it out onto a floured surface. Cut into golf-ball-size pieces and roll into tight balls. Rest them on the counter, covered, for 10 to15 minutes while you prepare the frying oil.

4. Fill a heavy-bottomed saucepan with 4 to 5 inches oil (enough so dough balls float). Heat to 350°F (test temperature with a small bit of dough—it should bubble immediately when it hits the oil). Fry until golden brown on all sides, 3 to 5 minutes. Drain on paper towels and serve dusted with powdered sugar.

Washington Irving

Sleepy Hollow Silverside of Beef (Corned Beef)

Serves 4-6

"The Legend of Sleepy Hollow" was based on real events—sort of. Sleepy Hollow and the surrounding areas of the Hudson River were settled by the Dutch in the early seventeenth century. During the Revolution, nearby Tarrytown where Washington Irving lived, was a hotbed of action. The British occupied the area to the south, and the region was full of outlaws, especially Hessian Jaegers—mercenaries known for their sharpshooting, horsemanship, and raids of Patriot camps. During one such raid, a Hessian was found without his head and was buried by the residents of Sleepy Hollow in the Old Dutch cemetery. He was the original Headless Horseman.

The Dutch oven, a cast-iron lidded pan originally made with feet to raise it over the coals, was named for the Dutch process of casting iron in sand. The flat Dutch oven lid, with a lip designed to hold coals, was Paul Revere's idea. It was the most-used cookware of the colonial period, and is still preferred today for long baking and braising because the heavy iron conducts heat slowly and evenly.

The silverside comes from the hindquarter of a cow, just below the rump and above the leg. It is lean with a wide grain, which benefits from slow, moist cooking, making it the perfect cut for corned beef. The name is a reference to the shiny silver membrane on one side of the cut.

The "corn" in corned beef is an old term for grain, used here in reference to an antiquated expression, "a corn of salt," which is the original form of today's "grain of salt." There is plenty of pre-seasoned corned beef on the market, but they all taste the same. Mix it up a bit with this homemade spice mix. A little originality goes a long way.

1 tablespoon whole coriander seeds
1 tablespoon whole mustard seeds
1 tablespoon black peppercorns
1 tablespoon paprika
1 tablespoon onion powder
1 tablespoon garlic powder
1 tablespoon brown sugar
One 3- to 5-pound silverside or beef brisket, trimmed of fat and membrane
2 tablespoons olive oil
1 onion, roughly chopped
2 large carrots, cut into large chunks
4 cloves garlic, minced
4 large red potatoes, quartered
2 teaspoons liquid smoke
1½-2 cups beer or cider

1. Preheat oven to 350°F. In a dry sauté pan, toast coriander and mustard seeds until fragrant. Cool slightly, then combine with peppercorns and grind in a coffee mill or mortar. Combine ground whole spices with paprika, onion and garlic powders, and brown sugar. Mix thoroughly. Take half of the spice mix and rub it thoroughly into the meat. Cover and refrigerate for 2 to 3 hours (or overnight).

2. Heat oil in a large Dutch oven. Add the beef. Brown on both sides, 1 to 2 minutes per side. Remove the browned meat and set aside. To the same pot, add onion and carrots. Cook until they begin to brown. Add garlic, potatoes, liquid smoke, the remaining spice mix, and beer, so that it just covers the vegetables, then bring the liquid to a boil.

3. Place meat on top of vegetables, cover the Dutch oven, and place in the oven. Bake for 60 to 90 minutes, adding liquid as necessary to keep moist. Remove meat from pot. Rest for 10 minutes before slicing.

Washington Irving

Rip Van Winkle's Catskill Sip Home-Brewed Hard Cider

Makes 1 gallon

Washington Irving first visited Tarrytown, New York, and neighboring Sleepy Hollow, on a trip up the Hudson River as a teenager, sent out of the city to avoid a yellow fever epidemic. These trips also took him to the nearby Catskill Mountains region, which he found a bit spooky and would later inspire his tale of "Rip Van Winkle."

Rip Van Winkle was a lazy Dutch settler who wandered into the hills to escape his naggy wife. He came upon a group of men dressed in old-fashioned clothes playing ninepins (old-time bowling). They gave him a brew to enjoy, and he soon fell asleep. When Rip woke up his beard was long, his gun was rusted, and his dog was gone. Twenty years had passed since he fell asleep, and it soon became clear that he had missed the American Revolutionary War, and that the men playing ninepins were the ghosts of Henry Hudson's crew. The legend remains, and everyone knows, that when you hear thunder in the Catskill Mountains, it's really a game of ninepins still being played. This recipe for home-brewed cider will not take twenty years to brew, but it does require some patience.

1 gallon glass jug (carboy), with rubber stopper and airlock
Funnel
Strainer
Four 1-quart swing-top bottles or growlers
Bleach water (1 tablespoon bleach to 1 gallon of water) or commercial sanitizing solution
1 gallon fresh-pressed apple juice
One 5-gram packet champagne or ale yeast

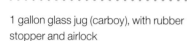

1. Clean everything that will touch the cider with soap and water, then sanitize it by submerging in bleach water for 2 minutes or by using a commercial sanitizer. Air-dry.

2. Pour juice into jug. Add yeast. Fill airlock with water to line indicated, attach it to the stopper, and insert the stopper into the jug. Set the jug aside at room temperature. The yeast will begin to feed on the sugar of the juice. The by-product from this feeding is carbon dioxide (CO_2, this is the same principle at work in bread making). Soon, bubbles will begin forming, with CO_2 escaping through the airlock. For the first 3 days, swirl the bottle every day to distribute the yeast and sugars. Fermentation will be complete when the yeast has consumed all the sugar, when there are no more bubbles being produced. This can take anywhere from 1 to 2 weeks. When the bubbles stop, give the sediment a chance to settle.

3. Strain cider from sediment and funnel into sanitized swing-top bottles. Set aside for another 1 to 2 weeks at room temperature to develop the carbonation. To check the carbonation, open one bottle carefully over a sink. If it meets your approval, refrigerate to stop the fermentation. If it needs more bubbles, leave it at room temperature for another few days.

Salem's Flying Ointment (Chicken Rillettes)

Serves 6-8

In the spring of 1692, two young girls in the village of Salem, Massachusetts, began screaming, barking, and dancing in the woods. Soon other girls exhibited similar behavior, and doctors diagnosed them with bewitchment. It was believed their Caribbean slave, Tituba, had performed black magic on them. Tituba confessed, then accused others in the hope that informing would lessen her sentence. More were accused of witchcraft, who in turn confessed and named others. A special court was convened, presided over by John Hathorne. Twenty suspects died by hanging, pressed by stones, or while in jail, but Minister Cotton Mather warned of insubstantial evidence. By 1693, the court was deemed unlawful, and the trials were over. In the 1970s, the girls' behavior was attributed to ergot, a parasitic fungus found in grain crops.

There is a long history of witchcraft in Europe, which would have been well known to the settlers. Old women making herbal remedies were often targeted, especially if they were cantankerous. One such remedy, Flying Ointment, was said to send users airborne if ingested or rubbed on the body. It was similar in scope to the way shamans use hallucinogens, producing a flying feeling rather than actual flight. The ointment here is meant to be smeared on crackers or slices of baguette. A cross between pâté and terrine, a rillette is spreadable, but with texture. It won't make you fly, but it is delicious.

1 yellow onion, roughly chopped
1 stalk celery, roughly chopped
1 medium carrot, roughly chopped
1 pound pork belly or bacon
1 large chicken, cut into pieces
Water as needed
2 bay leaves
4-5 sprigs each of fresh thyme, fresh sage, and fresh parsley, wrapped in a bouquet garni
1¼ teaspoons sea salt, divided
½ teaspoon freshly ground white pepper
1 teaspoon freshly grated nutmeg
Grated zest of 1 lemon
1 to 2 tablespoons white wine vinegar
4 tablespoons unsalted butter
2 tablespoons chopped fresh parsley

1. Preheat oven to 250°F. Mix onion, celery, and carrot in a large roasting pan and spread into an even layer. Place pork belly and chicken on top. Add enough water to come 1 inch up the sides and add bay leaves and bouquet garni. Cover tightly with foil or a lid. Braise in the oven for 2 to 3 hours, until the meat is tender and falls easily off the bone. Remove from oven. Cool until easily handled.

2. Skim 1 cup fat from pan and reserve. Strain and reserve cooking juices. Remove herbs. Shred meat with hands or two forks. When all meat is removed from the bone, break it down further, using forks or a potato masher. Add ½ cup of the reserved fat and about ½ to ¾ cup cooled-but-still-liquid cooking juice. Continue to mash. Add more fat or liquid as necessary for meat paste to be spreadable.

3. Season with 1 teaspoon of the salt, white pepper, nutmeg, lemon zest, and vinegar. Adjust seasoning. Pack into serving ramekins or jars.

4. Melt butter over medium heat. Pour on top of packed jars in a thin layer (just be sure all meat is covered). Garnish with fresh parsley and a sprinkle of salt, then chill until set, about an hour. Rillettes age well and can last a week in the fridge. Bring to room temperature for about an hour before serving with sliced baguette.

VARIATIONS
Try rabbit, duck, or venison. You'll need to add extra fat to leaner cuts, such as mashing in a few tablespoons of butter, to reach the desired consistency. This can also be made with salmon, though it needs less cooking time. Salmon rillettes is great as a schmear on a bagel.

Nathaniel Hawthorne

Seven Gables West Indies Spiced Duck

Serves 4

Nathaniel Hawthorne came from a long line of Salem residents, drawing on that history in his novels, which include *The House of the Seven Gables* and *The Scarlet Letter*. Like Washington Irving, he wrote mainly American characters in familiar American settings. Like other authors of the period, his work incorporated darker elements of the human experience. In representing the New England colonies, his message was sharply anti-Puritan and rich with moral metaphor.

The House of the Seven Gables is about past witchcraft, featuring a depressing house with a looming curse, mysterious deaths, and a wrongful accusation. It's fiction, but the house is real, and Hawthorne's own relative, John Hathorne, inspired the story. Presiding judge of the infamous Salem witch trials, Hathorne refused to repent his actions there. These events inspired an overarching theme of fate and the difficulty in escaping one's family's past. It also explores the social class structure of the period and the effects of depression. Hawthorne's work was highly influential and had a deep impact on both H. P. Lovecraft and Herman Melville.

The House of the Seven Gables is a real house, the Turner-Ingersoll mansion, which is still standing in Salem. Built in 1668, its residents were mariner merchants trading with the West Indies in commodities, including cod, lumber, sugar, textiles, spices, and pepper. After the American Revolution, ships from the port of Salem were the first from America to trade with the East Indies, and by the late eighteenth century, they were trading with China, Africa, Russia, and Australia. This dish is a reflection of that global trade, highly spiced and sweetened with molasses. Colonial cooks would have made this with a goose, which you can certainly do, but you're more likely to find a duck in your local market. If neither one is available, there's always turkey.

2 teaspoons whole allspice
2 teaspoons whole coriander
2 teaspoons black peppercorns
1 cinnamon stick
1 tablespoon paprika
1 teaspoon dried thyme
1 teaspoon ground ginger
4 duck legs
¼ cup molasses
2 tablespoons balsamic vinegar
1 teaspoon salt

1. In a dry skillet, toast allspice, coriander seeds, peppercorns, and cinnamon stick until fragrant. Cool. Grind to a fine powder in a coffee mill or mortar. Combine with paprika, thyme, and ginger in a small bowl.

2. Pat duck legs dry. Rub spice mix into meat. Place in zip-top bag. Refrigerate to marinate for 4 to 6 hours.

3. Preheat oven to 400°F and line a baking pan with a roasting rack. Set the marinated legs on the rack, skin-side up (duck has very fatty skin, so the rack allows the fat to drip down, which will make the skin crispy). Fill the bottom of the pan with 1 inch of water, to help prevent smoking. Cover with foil and roast for 30 minutes.

4. Combine molasses and vinegar in a small bowl. Remove the foil and brush the duck with the molasses mixture. Sprinkle with salt, then return to the oven uncovered. Continue roasting another 30 minutes, or until internal temperature reaches 180°F and the skin is crispy. Serve with roasted sweet potatoes or yams.

Index

N

O

About the Author

Leslie Bilderback is a classically trained chef, Certified Master Baker (CMB), culinary instructor, food writer, and culinary historian. She also holds a masters degree in art history, lecturing in art at local state and community colleges.

She received her classic European culinary training in the 1980s at the California Culinary Academy, and worked in several well-regarded restaurants, including Postrio in San Francisco, and most recently Michelin starred n/naka in Los Angeles. She has been executive chef for Le Cordon Bleu USA, taught in the Los Angeles Unified School District's Nutrition Network program, and taught culinary arts all over the world for the United States Navy. In addition, she participated as a contestant on, and then won, Food Network's *Sweet Genius* (season 3, episode 9, "Dream-Catching Genius").

She's written many cookbooks, including five books for St. Martin's Press (*Salt*, September 2016, *Mug Meals*, September 2015, *No-Churn Ice Cream*, May 2015, *The Spiralized Kitchen*, March 2015, and *Mug Cakes*, August 2013), two books for Adams Media (*The Everything Bread Book*, August 2010, *The Everything Family Nutrition Book*, August 2008), and eight titles for Penguin's Alpha Books (*The Complete Idiot's Guide to Sensational Salads*, July 2009, *The Complete Idiot's Guide to Snack Cakes*, June 2008, *The Complete Idiot's Guide to Good Food from the Good Book*, March 2008, *The Complete Idiot's Guide to Spices and Herbs*, December 2007, *The Complete Idiot's Guide to Comfort Food*, September 2007, and *The Complete Idiot's Guide to Success as a Chef*, February 2007). She was also the ghostwriter for Sherry Yard's 2004 James Beard Award winning book *The Secrets of Baking*, Houghton Mifflin, 2003, and penned *100th Year, Sun Maid Raisins and Dried Fruits* for DK Publishing, 2011. In addition, she wrote a monthly food column in the *Arroyo Magazine* for twelve years.